Dick Bruna

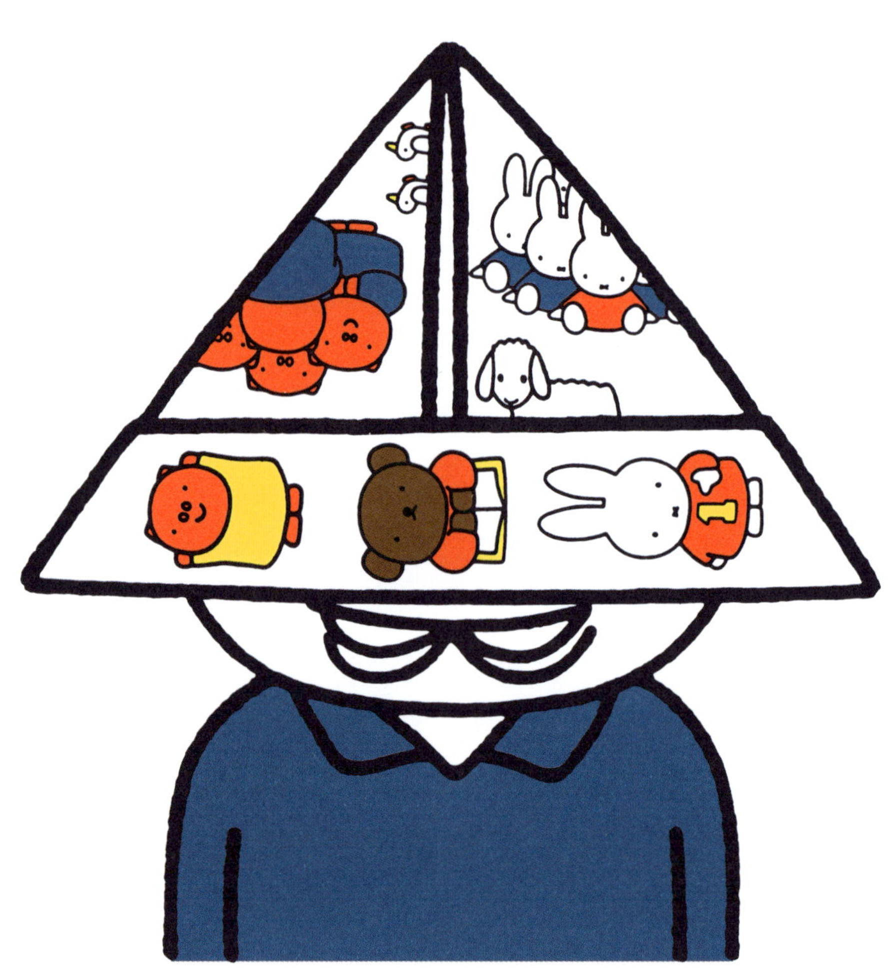

Bruce Ingman and
Ramona Reihill

Dick Bruna

SERIES CONSULTANT QUENTIN BLAKE
SERIES EDITOR CLAUDIA ZEFF

116 ILLUSTRATIONS

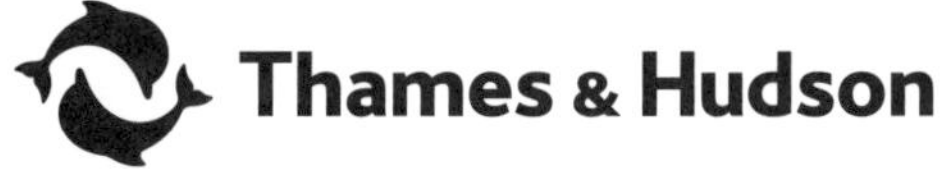

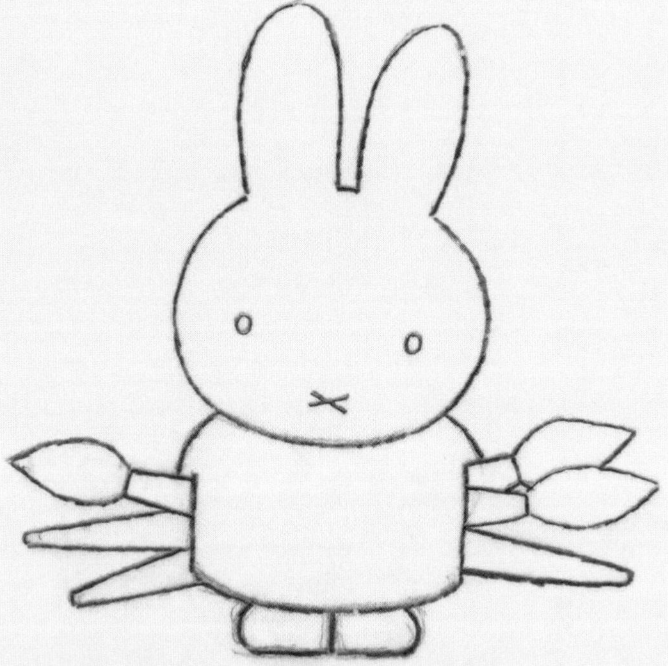

FRONT COVER Uncle Pilot, from *Miffy Goes Flying*, 1970
BACK COVER Dick Bruna at work, photograph by Ferry
André de la Porte © copyright Mercis bv

FRONTISPIECE Self-portrait, 1991
ABOVE *Miffy at the Gallery*, 1997
PAGE 112 Silkscreen print, 2002

Dick Bruna © 2020 Thames & Hudson Ltd, London
Text © 2020 Bruce Ingman
Illustrations Dick Bruna © copyright Mercis bv, 1953–2020
BLACK BEAR © copyright Dick Bruna
Publication licensed by Mercis Publishing bv, Amsterdam

Designed by Therese Vandling

First published in 2020 the United States of America by
Thames & Hudson Inc., 500 Fifth Avenue, New York,
New York 10110

www.thamesandhudsonusa.com

Library of Congress Control Number 2019947782

ISBN 978-0-500-09413-6

Printed and bound in China by Leo Paper Products Ltd

CONTENTS

Introduction

In the summer of 1955, Dick Bruna, his wife Irene and their
one-year-old son, Sierk, went on a holiday to the seaside,
their first as a family. They rented a small house with a
garden that ran down to the sea in the Northern Dutch
town of Egmond aan Zee. One day, in a scene not unlike
one in a picture book, the family watched as a little rabbit
scampered into the sand dunes. Not long after, as Sierk has
been reminded countless times, the bunny made it into his
bedtime stories. And, soon after they returned home, Bruna
drew the little rabbit for his son. 'Because I was an artist
I thought it might be nice to try and draw the rabbit.'[1]

Every story has a beginning and this is Miffy's. But it is
not the beginning of Bruna's artistic story; he had been an
aspiring artist and graphic designer for some time and he
had already published a book in 1953, *The Apple*. In fact,
Dick Bruna's life in books began on the day he was born into
a successful Dutch publishing family. His love of art, and
desire to be an artist, permeated every day of his life.

Today, his books, illustrations, book covers and posters
have been shown internationally; there's always a Bruna
exhibition on somewhere in the world. He is regarded as
one of his country's greatest ever artists, ranked alongside
Johannes Vermeer and Piet Mondrian. He is hailed as a
hero of the clear line, the 'klare lijn', and celebrated as one
of the Netherlands most translated authors, second only
to Anne Frank. An exact replica of Bruna's studio is now
a permanent exhibit in the Centraal Museum in Utrecht.
Across the street, Miffy has her own museum and is patron
of the prize for the world's best children's museum.
By the time of Bruna's death in 2017, the thirty-two Miffy
books had been translated into more than fifty languages
in eighty-five countries and had generated a spin-off
industry that includes television, stage musicals and
a multi-million-pound global merchandising business.

So, to the beginning . . .

Birth and early days

Bruna was born in the central Dutch city of Utrecht on 23 August 1927 to Johanna Clara Charlotte Erdbrink and Albert Willem (Abs) Bruna, and christened Hendrik Magdalenus Bruna after his grandfather. By some quirk of fate, not lost on Bruna himself, it happened to be the Year of the Rabbit in the Chinese Zodiac. His father ran the successful publishing company, A. W. Bruna & Zoon, founded by his great-grandfather in 1868. By the turn of the century they owned a book kiosk in almost every train station in the Netherlands. As the first born of a first-born son who had taken over running the family business from his father,

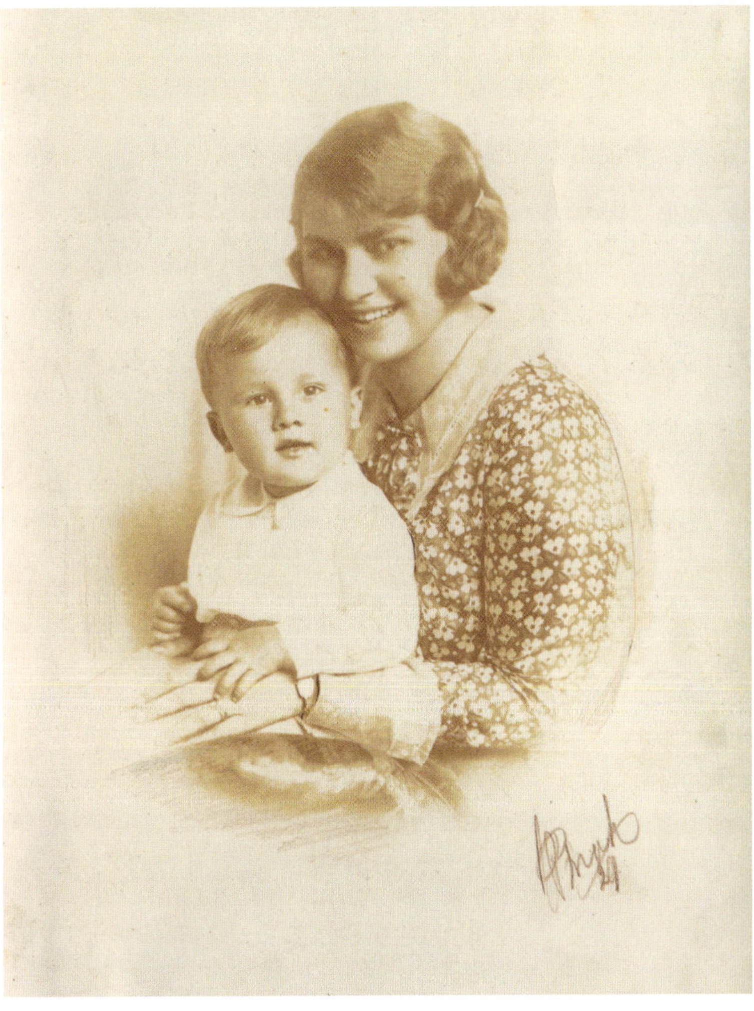

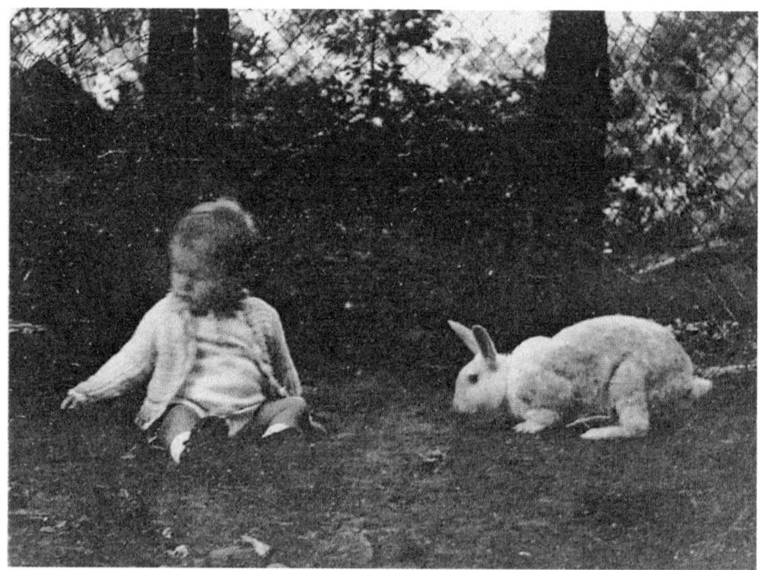

Bruna's succession was assumed. Certainly, as far as his father was concerned, a career in publishing was not only his destiny but also his duty. Tradition demanded it of him. Bruna knew this from an early age but it did not prevent him from thinking otherwise.

Hendrik was a quiet, plump baby, affectionately referred to as Dik or Dikkie (fat or fatty), the name that stuck. Born with club feet, the treatment and extra attention this required may help explain his particular devotion to his mother. Having to sit still for long periods, he learned to entertain himself by reading quietly and daydreaming, a talent he would proudly never lose.

In 1931, Bruna's brother, Frederik Hendrik (Frits), was born. Soon after, the family moved to a large house in Zeist, a town east of Utrecht popular with wealthy families from the city. For the Bruna brothers it was idyllic, a bucolic dream. There was a playroom and a summerhouse and a garden where chickens, rabbits, dogs and even an excitable goat wandered freely. In the summer, they played in their toy cars and were allowed to ride in the goat cart as their mother ran protectively alongside. In the winter, they learned to skate on a homemade ice rink and even set up a makeshift ski run. Their grandparents lived nearby in the affluent woodland village of Bosch en Duin with a similarly extensive garden of toys and animals including one larger-than-life white rabbit. If all of this seems familiar to Miffy readers, it's because it is. Miffy lives in a world very similar to that experienced by Dick and Frits.

Life in Zeist was also filled with music and books. There were piano lessons and they listened to the radio and a wide range of music on the gramophone. Bruna developed a lifelong passion for the French chanson, almost to the exclusion of any other music. Authors and designers came

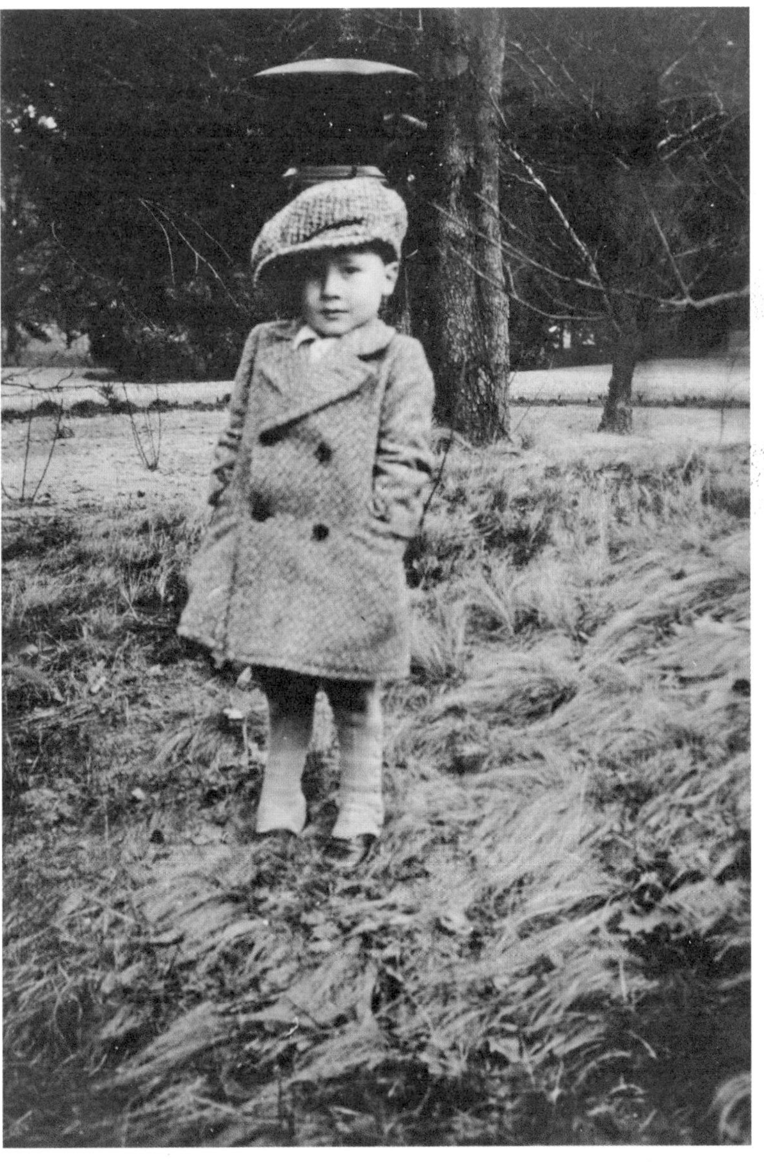

Bruna aged 5

to visit regularly. The boys were read to and Bruna enjoyed
all sorts of books, from poetry to adventure stories. He loved
Dutch hero books and the Babar stories by Jean de Brunhoff,
and at secondary school secretly read comic books that were
frowned upon at that time.

This was a childhood of freedom, security and culture in
a liberal Protestant household.

Even as political tensions increased across Europe, and
many suffered from the hardships of a worldwide economic
depression, the skies remained clear over Zeist. Bruna only
ever remembered his life there as glorious.[2]

When he was 6, Bruna started at the Hernhutterschool, a
Moravian primary school chosen not for its creed but simply
because it was close to the Bruna home. There he learnt
Bible stories that came in useful when he wrote *Noah's Ark*
and *Christmas* but the young boy did not receive any zealous
teaching that would make a lasting impression.

> *The foundations of his artistry were laid at primary
> school. Dick was small, liked drawing, was good at
> Dutch, wrote essays or letters for other pupils but
> was also a quiet boy who liked to be alone and could
> busy himself for hours. In that respect, this wouldn't
> change throughout his life. He would spend hours
> alone in his studio using techniques that seemed to
> derive directly from primary school art class.[3]*

In early 1940 the family moved to the nearby town of
Bilthoven and Bruna attended the Het Nieuwe Lyceum.
Here, he learned to play the accordion and began to
entertain family and visitors with renditions of famous
French singers, in particular Charles Trenet, helped by
sheet music brought from Paris by his father. The older,
shyer Bruna would look back at his younger confident
self in amazement. 'That I dared do that at the time!'[4]
On the bookshelves at home, Bruna discovered books
about Rembrandt and Vincent van Gogh and he read
them, as he recalled, 'I think five or six times'.[5]

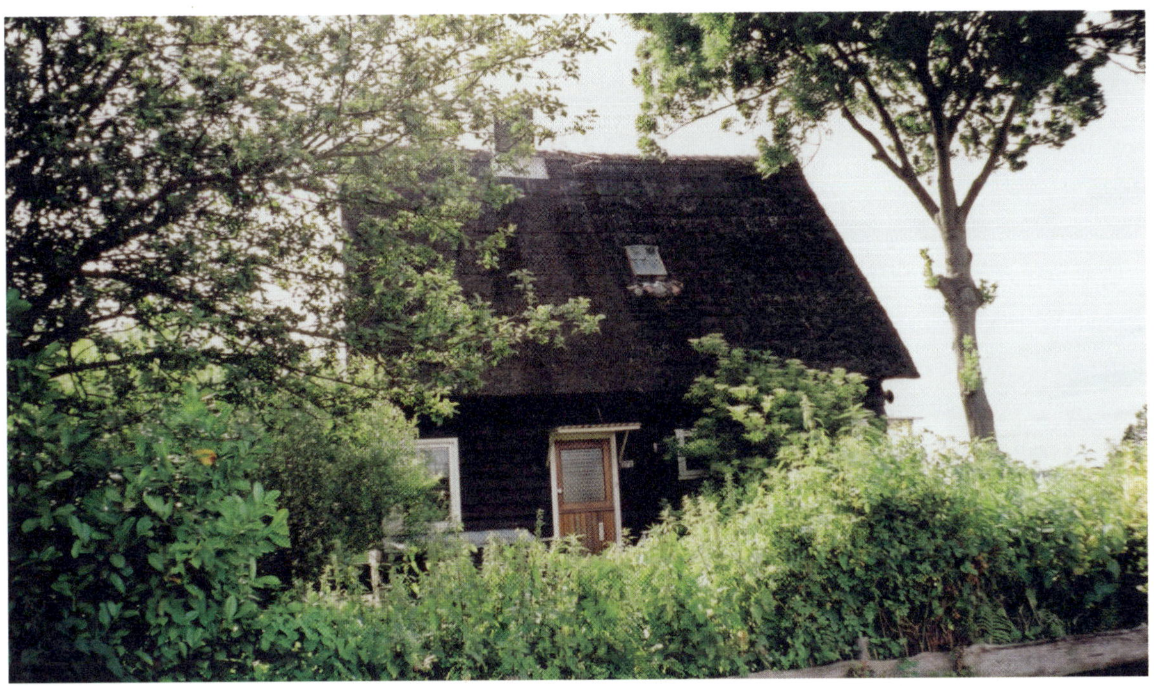

War years

In May of that same year, Nazi Germany launched an
attack on the Netherlands and Belgium. Holland's decades
of neutrality were at an end. But it wasn't until 1943 that
the conflict tearing through Europe finally had an impact
on the Bruna household when the German army confiscated
their house in Bilthoven. At 40 and 16, father and son risked
being taken into forced labour in Germany and so the family
decided to go into hiding at their summer retreat. Their
small lakeside house on the Loosdrechtse Plassen, an area
of interconnecting lakes south of Amsterdam, proved an
ideal setting for a dreamy adolescent and it is here that
the romantic side of Bruna emerged.

For Bruna, this new life was no imposed hardship; rather,
it provided extended hours of solitude for writing, drawing,
painting, composing songs, playing his accordion and, best
of all, dreaming: '...we had a pleasant time. I was already
sketching constantly: on any piece of paper I could get
hold of, I tried to make a little drawing.'[6] He even painted

ABOVE
The Bruna house in Breukelerveen,
Loosdrechtse Plassen (a lake
district near Amsterdam)

on abandoned bits of wood; old doors and shelves were appropriated for his landscape paintings.

Rein van Looy, a children's book illustrator well known for illustrating the first Dutch edition of *The Wonderful Wizard of Oz* and *Gulliver's Travels*, and a book cover designer for A. W. Bruna, regularly came to visit and would take Bruna out on the lake for drawing sessions. From their little rowing boat they sketched the world around them and then later, at home, Bruna would create oil paintings from his drawings. Sometimes he gave them to their neighbouring farmers in exchange for sugar or butter, rare wartime commodities.

But the teenage dreamer refused to hide when they came under threat of a German raid. He often had to be dragged away from his favourite daydreaming spot at the window. The German army didn't pose a big enough danger for the boy who was scared of the dark and didn't feel the need to crawl into a tiny spider-filled cupboard.

Father and son clashed constantly. They became ever more entrenched in their divergent views on Bruna's future: on one side Abs Bruna remained adamant that the responsibility of taking over the business belonged to the eldest son, on the other Bruna had no plan to do anything other than write and paint.

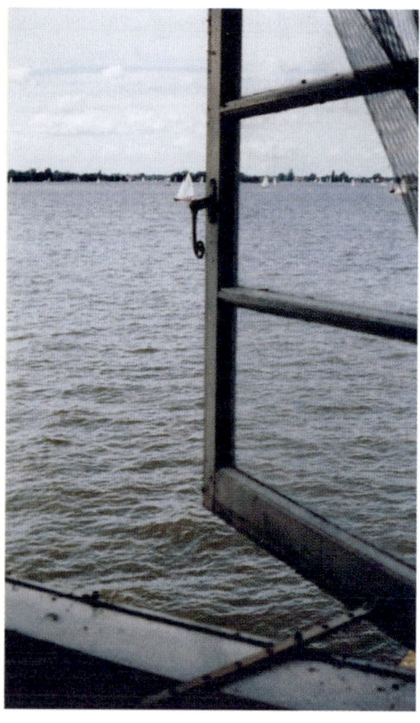
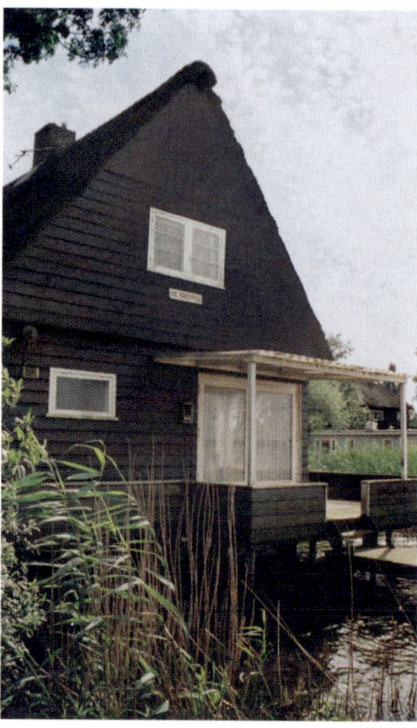

View from the window and the outside of the Bruna retreat on the Loosdrechtse Plassen

Bruna found it difficult to distinguish between protective parent and ambitious businessman; he didn't feel under threat from the Germans, only from his overbearing father. In turn, Abs Bruna was anxious about his family's safety and concerned about the business. (The publishing industry was badly affected by German censorship and a crisis in the paper industry during the war years.) Bruna would acknowledge years later that he had reached a better understanding of his father after he had his own children (though he never tried to impose his ambitions on them). He realized that he had been rebelling against everything that his father represented, which was the complete opposite of the future he wanted for himself. For now, all he could see was a kind, loving mother who created a lively home, singing and playing with the boys constantly, and a father who only nagged and badgered and, worse still, as Bruna discovered, had been unfaithful to his mother.

This emotional turmoil was revealed in a story Bruna wrote and illustrated entitled *Japie*, dedicated to his mother. Written as a fairy tale, it tells of a poor child who earns money for his sick mother by playing the accordion. His parents die and he is taken in by his wicked uncle and aunt; he runs away and is saved by an old farmer's wife

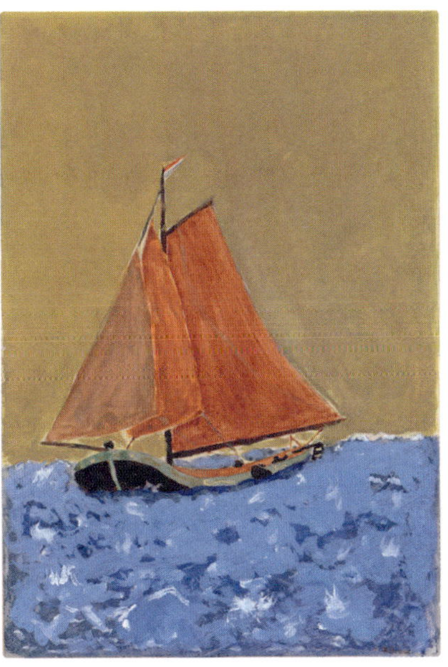

RIGHT
Early painting of a sailboat, 1943

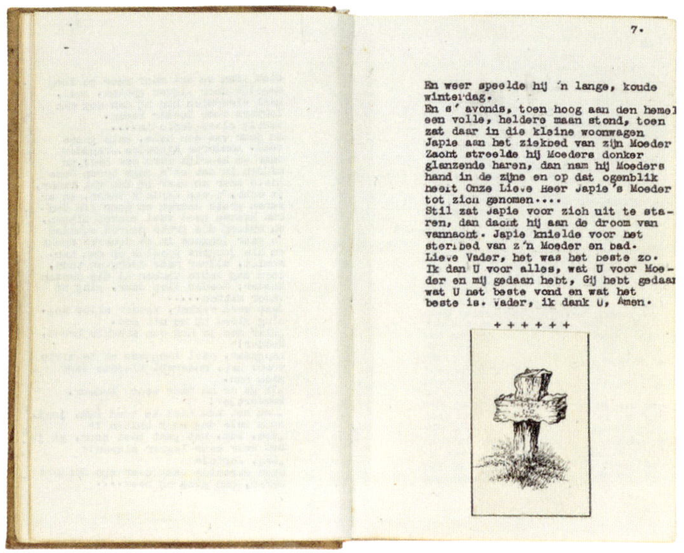
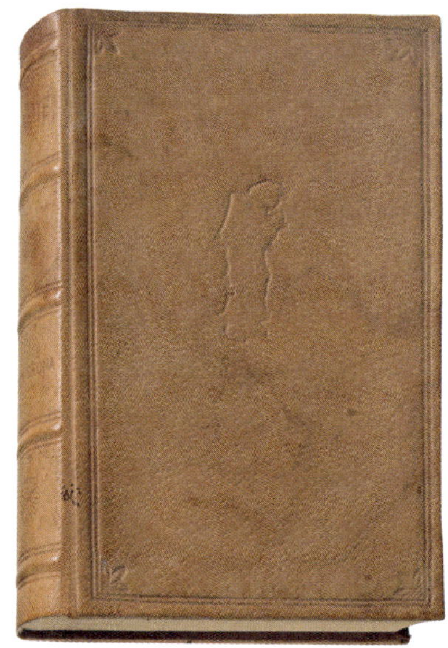

Last page and leather-bound
volume of self-published book,
Japie, 1943–45

and her daughter. In this tale of war, love and parental
misunderstanding, which Bruna later described as
'sentimental and also very pious, a preoccupation of mine
at that time', all ends happily.[7] The accompanying
pen-and-ink illustrations are reminiscent of the Dutch
painter and illustrator Anton Pieck and the illustrator Jo
Spier, both with styles typical of fairy tales. Although the
book has never been published, the original leather-bound
version still exists and it remains a good insight into the
mind of the brooding teenager.

London and Paris

In 1945, the Netherlands was fully liberated by Allied forces.
The Bruna family emerged from hiding and moved to the
large commuter town of Hilversum, where the occupying
German army had based their headquarters. The bunker
years had given Bruna the freedom to explore his creative
interests and the opportunity to educate himself. Now he
knew for sure that he wanted to write and draw. At first,
he reluctantly agreed to go to the local school but it was
difficult to revert to a routine. 'While it was a nice class,
two boys and two girls, and very convivial, I couldn't cope.'[8]

Although Bruna's father understood that his son 'wanted no more to do with school desks',[9] both of them clung to their opposing ambitions. While Bruna designed his first book cover for the Bruna publishing house, his father organized his practical publishing education. The book cover was for *Anne-Marie* by the Indonesian author Arnold Clerx. It is a gentle, atmospheric illustration, very similar in spirit to the work Bruna had been producing in hiding, a landscape with a pale blue wash over the top. Bruna's work experience began with a year in the Broese bookshop in Utrecht. There followed two year-long placements with the newsagent W. H. Smith in London and the publisher Plon in Paris.

Abs Bruna unerringly believed publishing was the family trade and art was a hobby that his son could pursue in his own time; what the businessman failed to grasp was that he was sending his son on an artistic odyssey that would intensify his passions.

Bruna soaked up everything the art world had to offer. 'I really went from one gallery to another all day.'[10] He discovered modern art. 'I saw Picasso for the first time and Léger and all those big painters. When I saw Matisse's work – especially his late collages – he became the most important man in my life.'[11] And Fernand Léger would have a lifelong effect on Bruna, particularly his use of line and

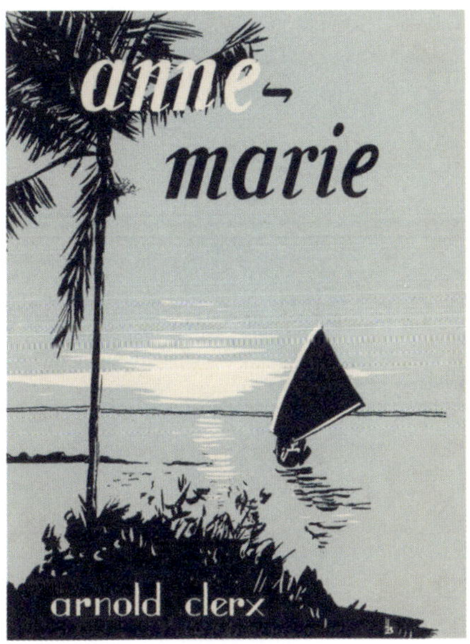

First book cover for A. W. Bruna,
1946

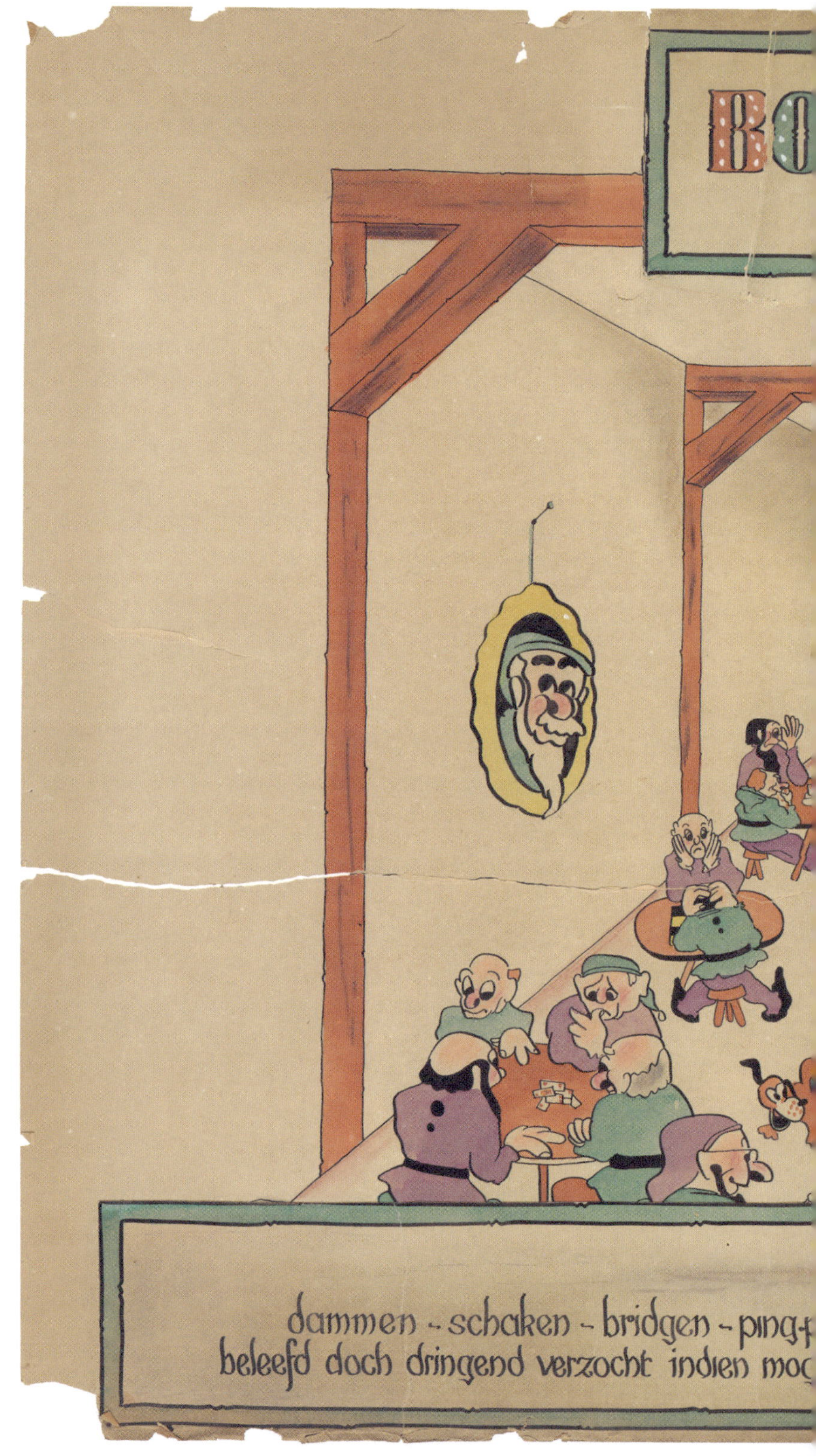

Illustration for games' night at
Het Nieuwe Lyceum High School
in Hilversum, *c.* 1946

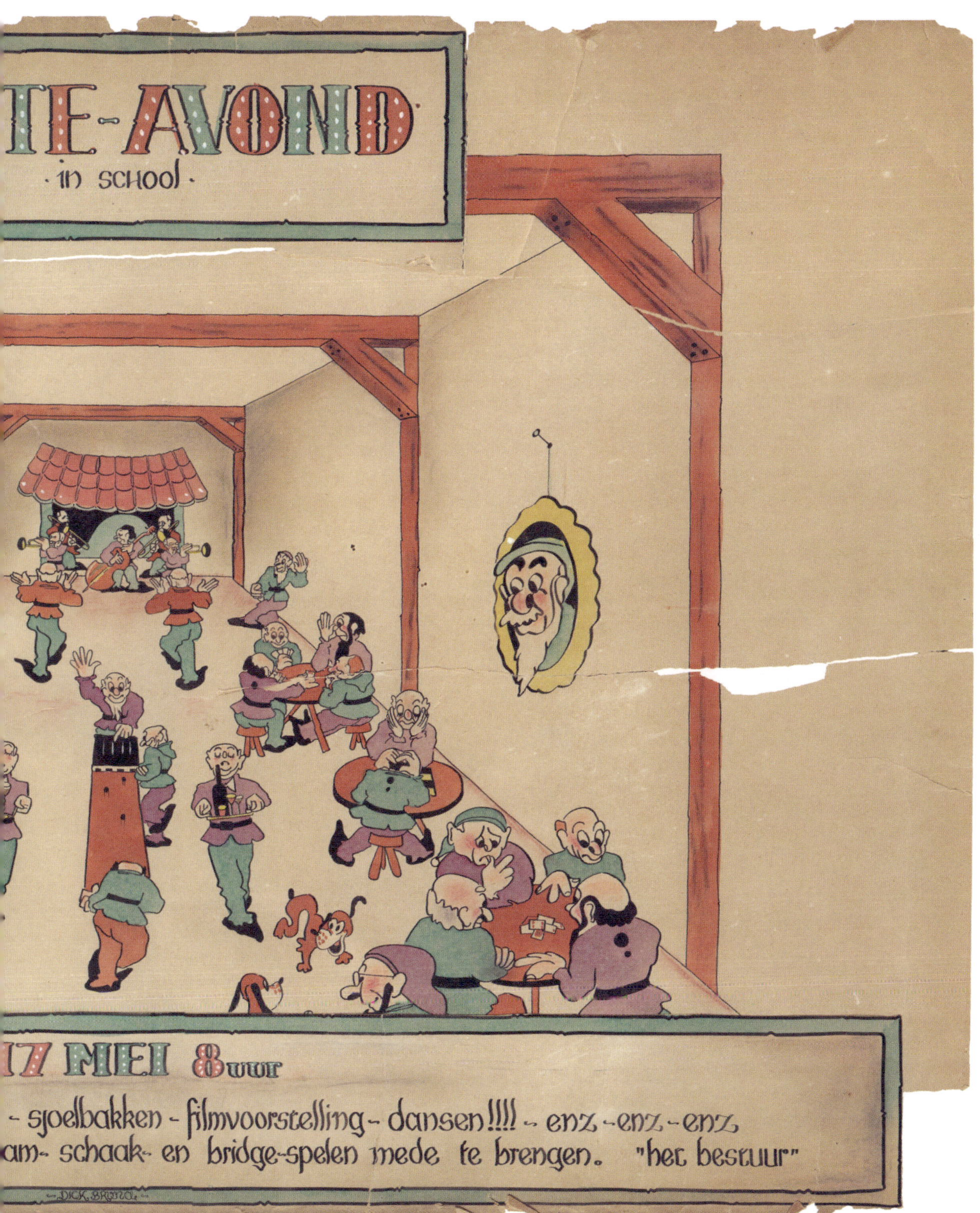
TE-AVOND
· in school ·
17 MEI 8 uur
- sjoelbakken - filmvoorstelling - dansen!!!! - enz - enz - enz
am- schaak- en bridge-spelen mede te brengen.   "het bestuur"
DICK BRUNA

colour. He realized that line, form, colour and perspective could all be manipulated or disregarded entirely. One didn't need to be constrained by convention and tradition.

In this period, Bruna resumed his habit of reading artists' biographies and pursued his love of French music including a particularly memorable trip to the London Palladium to see Maurice Chevalier. He sketched outdoors in a small sketchbook at every opportunity, keeping up the practice of drawing everything around him before developing them into oils on canvas at home. There wasn't a tourist spot in Paris he didn't visit, drawing street vendors and musicians, bridges and buildings. He made pen and pencil drawings and monochromes and oil paintings. These were heady times in the existentialist cafés of postwar Paris. The city was embracing all things American from jazz clubs to check shirts and Bruna would have felt the frisson of a capital realizing its freedom.

As his immersion in the world of modern art deepened, Bruna saw how colours worked with other colours to create something new; they could fill a space or create a new space. He understood the power of this and he would use his ability to conjure up colours to depict an atmosphere throughout his working life. Bruna's time in Paris was so inspiring and liberating that he would return to the city for at least a few days every year to re-energize, rekindle his inspiration and catch one of his favourite French singers in concert.

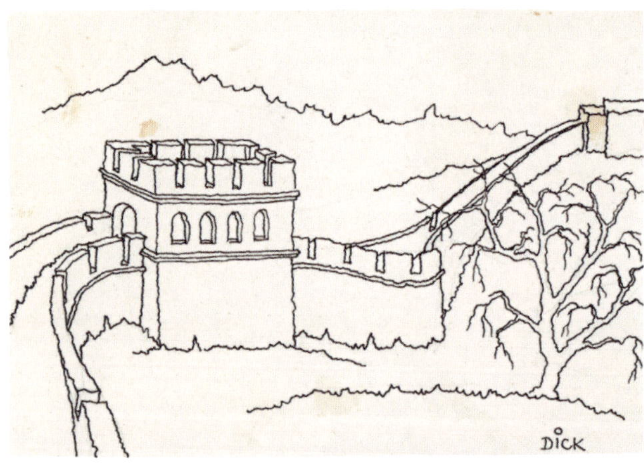

LEFT
Early drawing of the Great
Wall of China

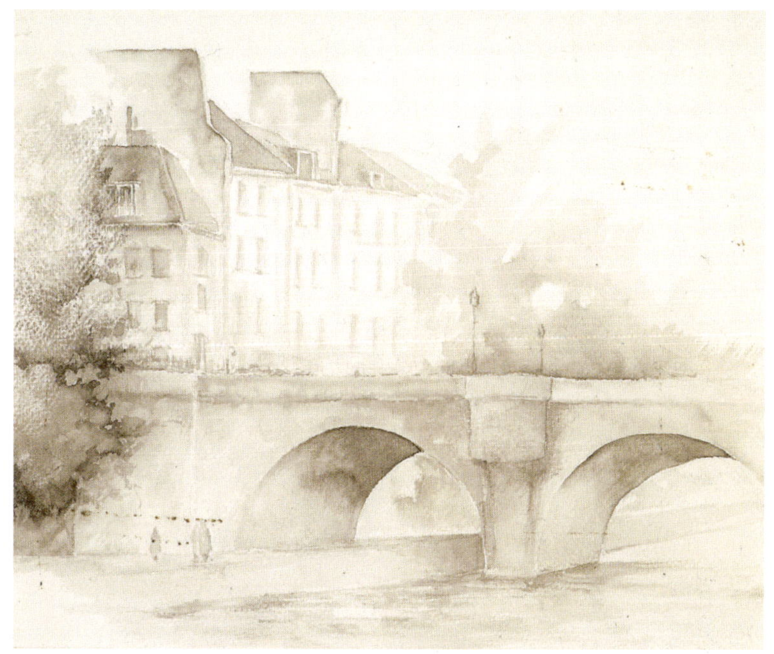

RIGHT
Pen, brush and wash drawing of a
bridge over the Seine, Paris, 1949

BELOW
Drawing, Paris, 1949

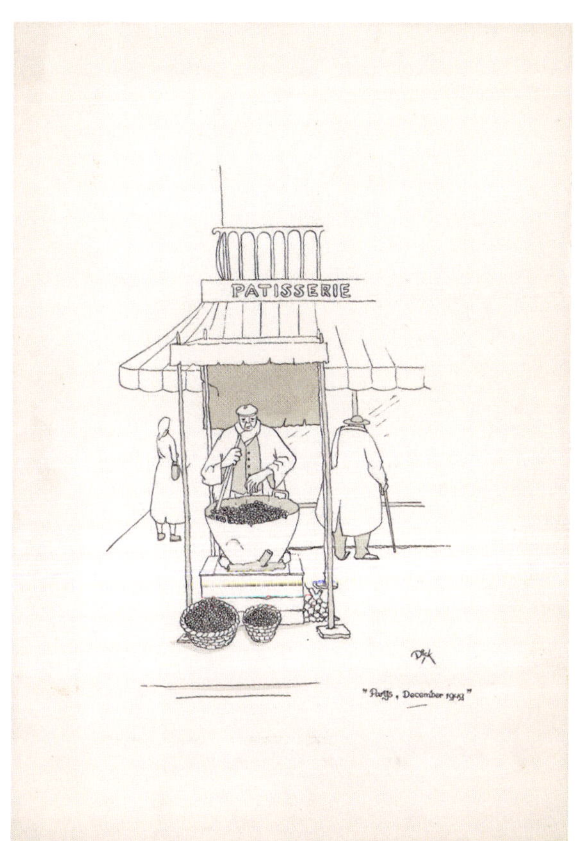

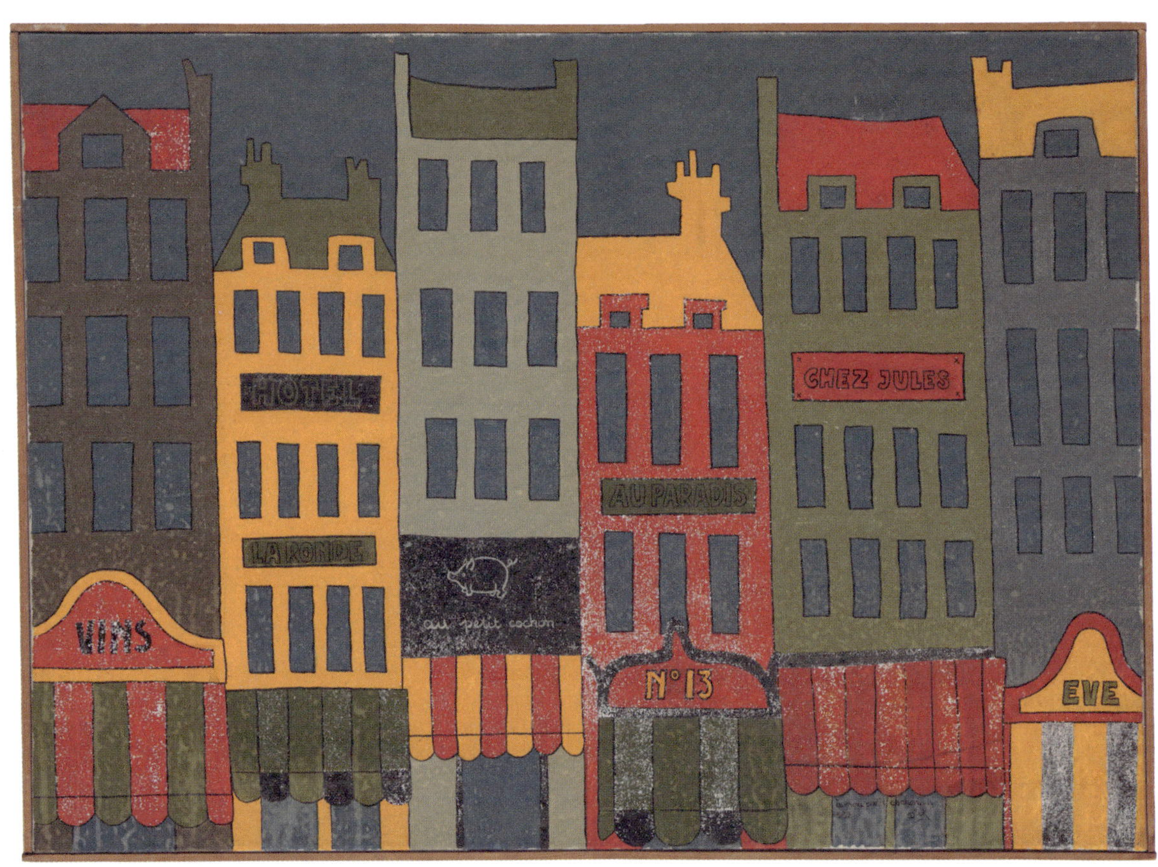

Paintings, early 1950s

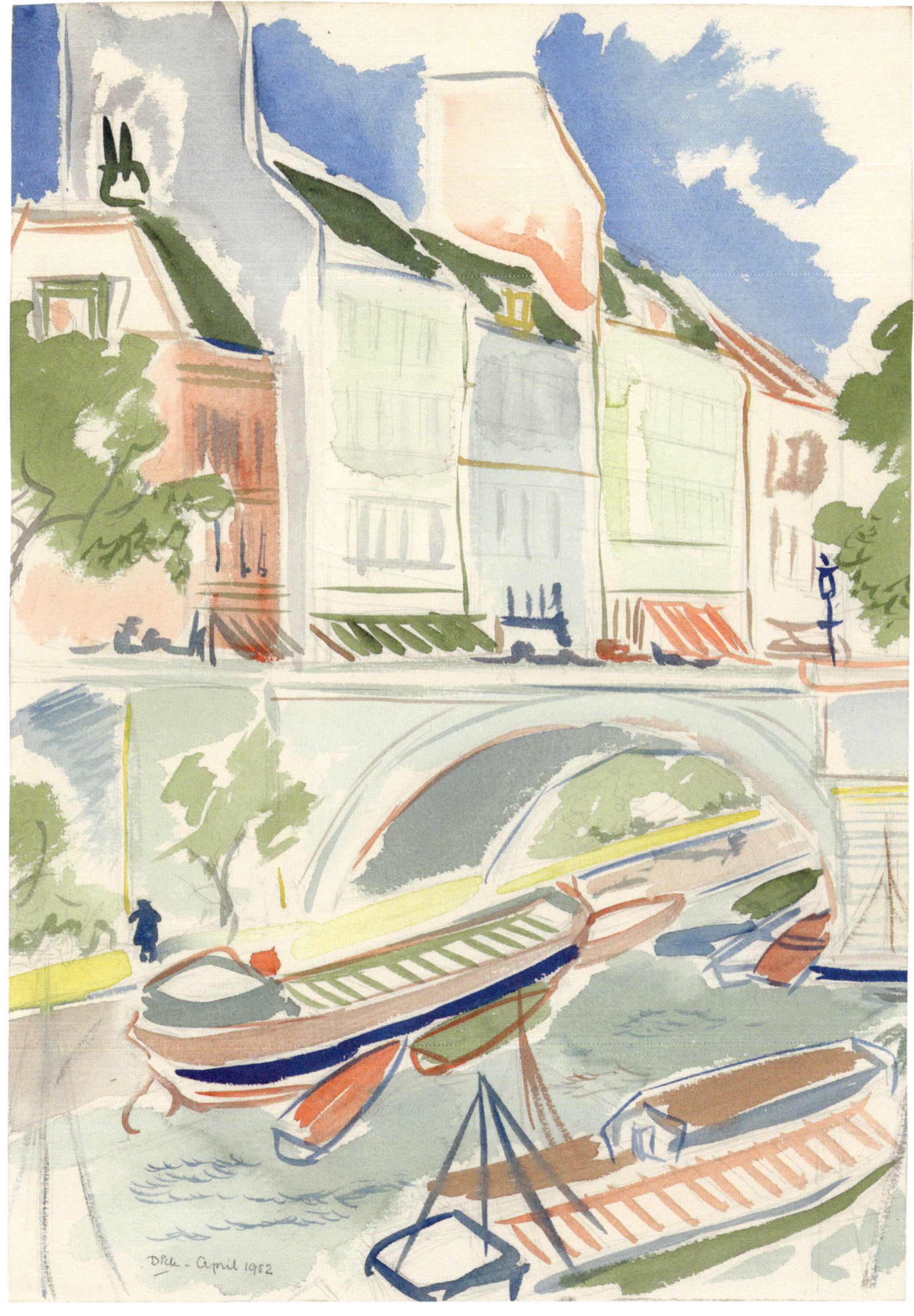
Dick - April 1952

The return

If Abs Bruna thought his son would return home prepared
to take on a business role in the company, he was wrong;
he was more determined than ever to be an artist. Bruna
had been thoroughly bored by his publishing education
but galvanized by his personal cultural enlightenment.
His passion for art was such that he was able to convince
his father that instead of starting work he needed to pursue
an art education. Surprisingly and with minimum drama,
it was agreed that he could go to the Rijksakademie, the
Academy of Visual Art in Amsterdam.

Bruna moved to the capital and took up a place under the
tutelage of Jos Rovers, an exponent of the 'people's painter'
George Hendrik Breitner, often referred to as one of the
Amsterdam Impressionists who depicted the everyday life
of the city. In the past this would have appealed to Bruna
but, once again, formal education proved too restrictive.
The direction of the course was darkly impressionistic,
a backward step for someone who had experienced the
galleries of London and Paris and the joy of sketching,
wherever, whenever, whatever he chose. He didn't want to
draw the dull grey plaster busts on offer here, he wanted
to know more about the convention-defying, modern
painters he had discovered, and he was impatient to get
back to drawing outdoors and experimenting with colour
and form. After six months, he abandoned the course.

With his artistic dreams intact, Bruna needed to earn
money so he started designing book covers for A. W. Bruna,
working from home. His early cover designs from 1950
to 1952 reveal his influences but no coherent style. There
were flirtations with his youthful interests, such as Walt
Disney and Jo Spier, and experiments based on his more
recent encounters with modernists, but mainly he was still
searching for his own idiom. He signed these covers HB, for
Henk Bruna, perhaps distancing himself from these designs,
saving his name for the artist he hoped to become?

Menu for place setting for Bruna,
showing the influence of Walt
Disney, for a company dinner,
Hotel Noord-Brabant, Utrecht,
1 March 1948

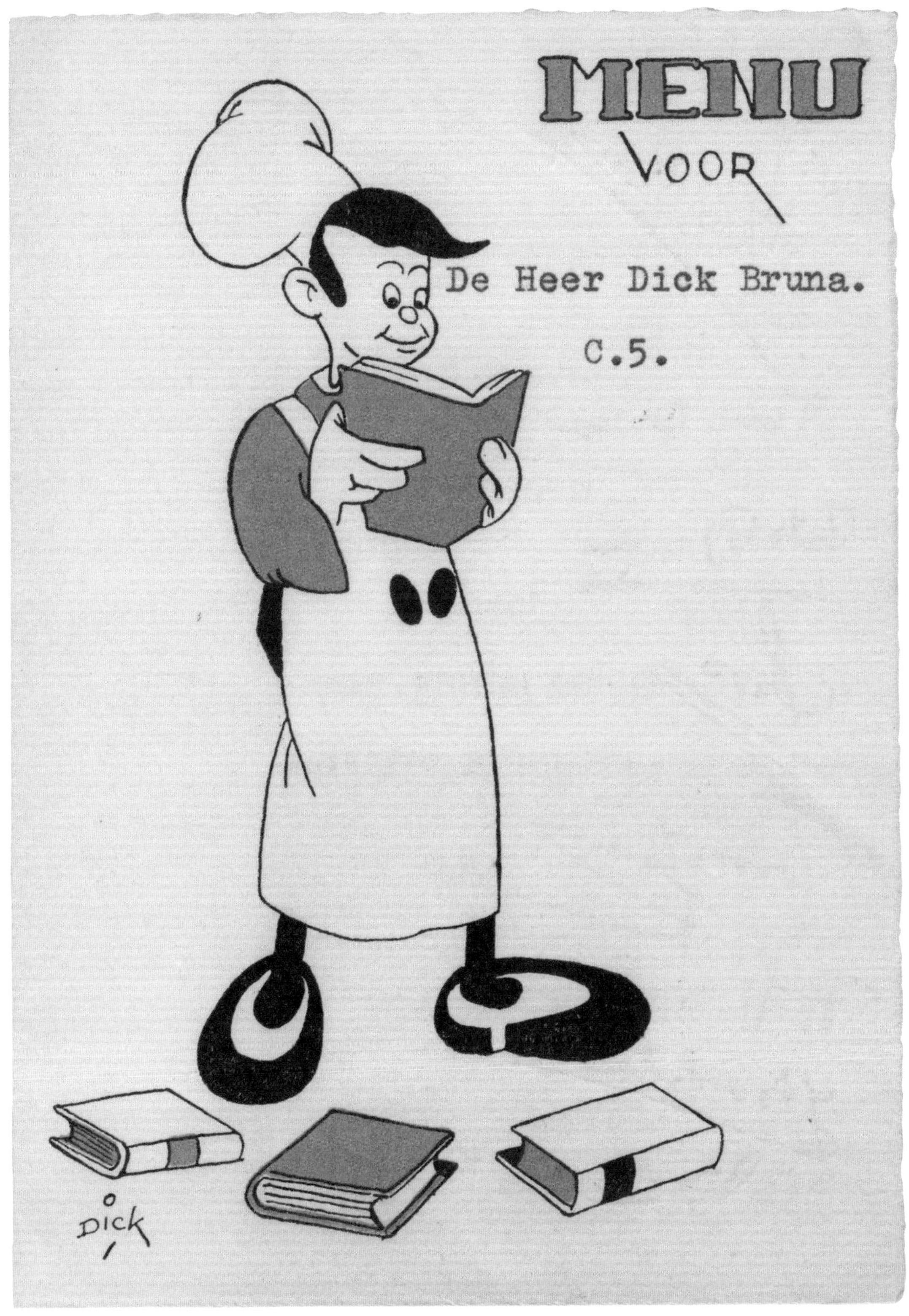
MENU
VOOR
De Heer Dick Bruna.
C.5.
DICK

Influences

As well as the work of Henri Matisse and Léger, Bruna loved
the De Stijl (The Style) movement, a group of Dutch artists
and architects who advocated the complete simplification
of composition to the essentials of form and colour: vertical
and horizontal forms using only black, white, grey and
primary colours. Initially he was influenced by the early
work of Bart van der Leck due to his more figurative
approach. 'He started from reality and tried to reduce it
to the most essential.'[12] Later he would look to Mondrian,
emulating the way he reduced reality to two dimensions.
But it was the work of Gerrit Rietveld with his devotion to
squares that proved most significant. The Rietveld-designed
Schröder House, built in Utrecht in 1924, and originally
commissioned to be designed without walls, was one of the
best-known examples of the De Stijl style. The house grew
increasingly more important to Bruna as he came to know
both it and the designer better.

Bruna in front of the Rietveld
Schröder House, Utrecht

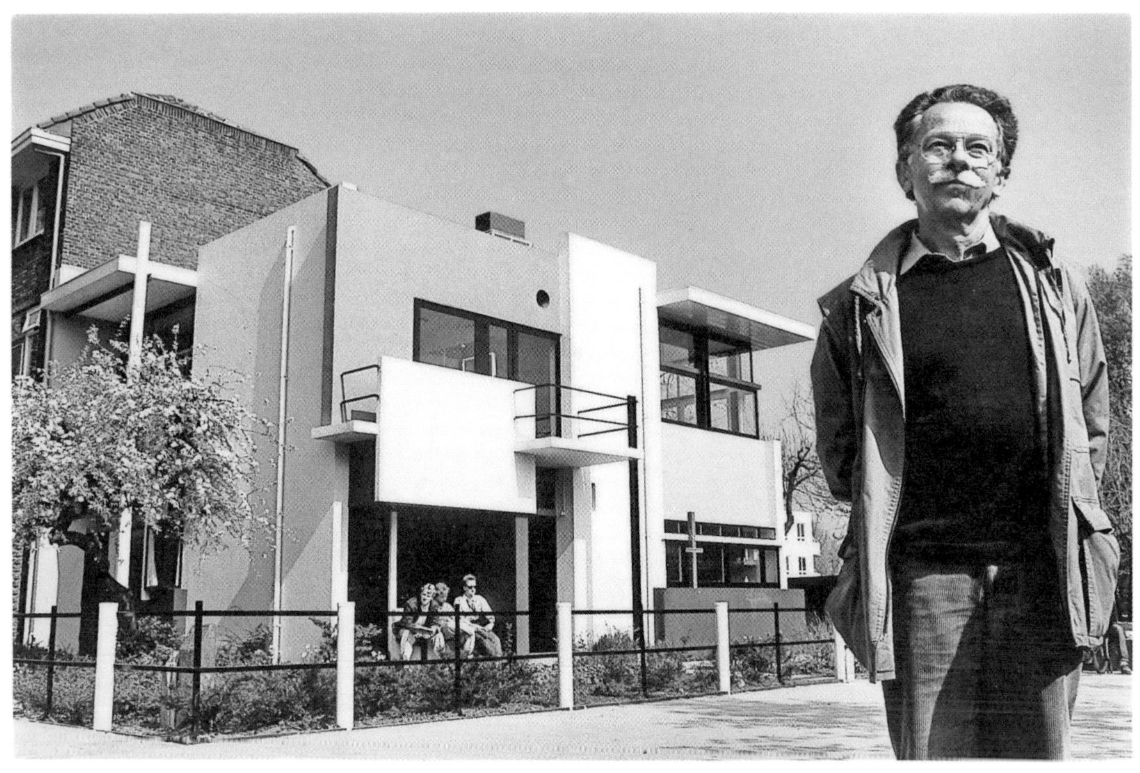

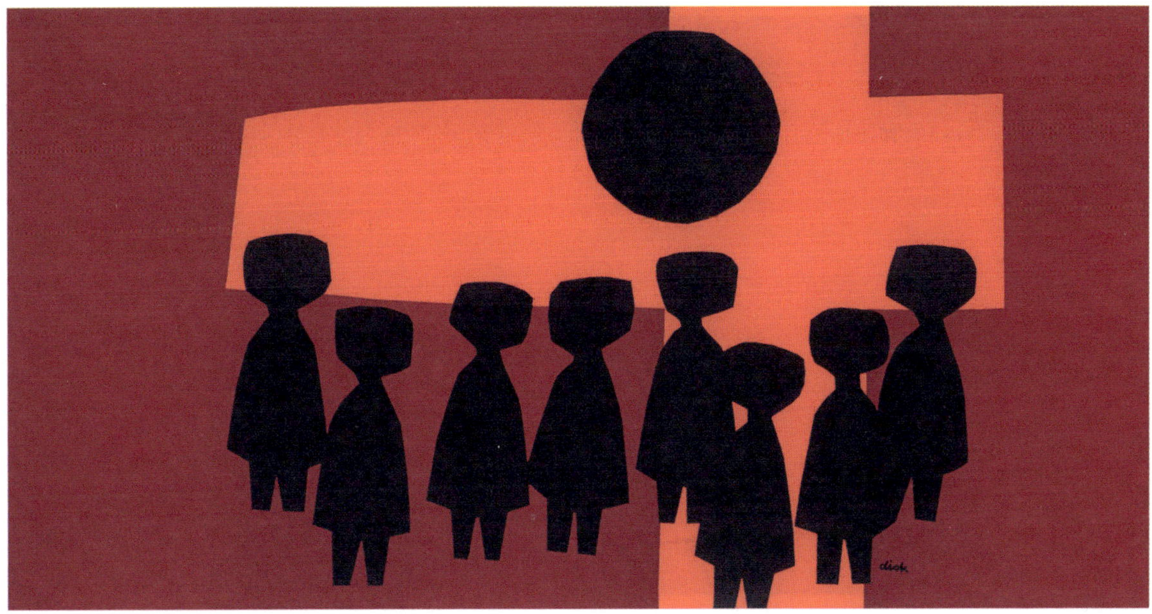

ABOVE
H. N. Werkman-inspired design for a book cover, 1961

PAGE 26
Programme for *Muziek van onze tijd* (Music of our time) for the 1958–59 concert season at Tivoli Lepelenburg in Utrecht, 1958

PAGE 27
Poster for the art exhibition *Chisel and Palette*, 150 years of Genootschap Kunstliefde, at the Centraal Museum, Utrecht, 1957

The artist and designer Willem Sandberg also provided modernist inspiration and, as the director of the Stedelijk Museum from 1945 to 1963, would introduce Bruna to modern art he may not otherwise have seen. Another influence was the stencilling work of Hendrik Nicolaas (H. N.) Werkman as evidenced on his later book cover designs. 'Werkman's Hassidic prints have been really important to me; they were totally direct and abstract things.'[13] Sandberg's own graphic design practice would have a more obvious impact in his choice of typeface on covers and books. Over the years, Bruna would distil all this inspiration until his work on covers, books and posters started to influence each other, in a form of cross-pollination.

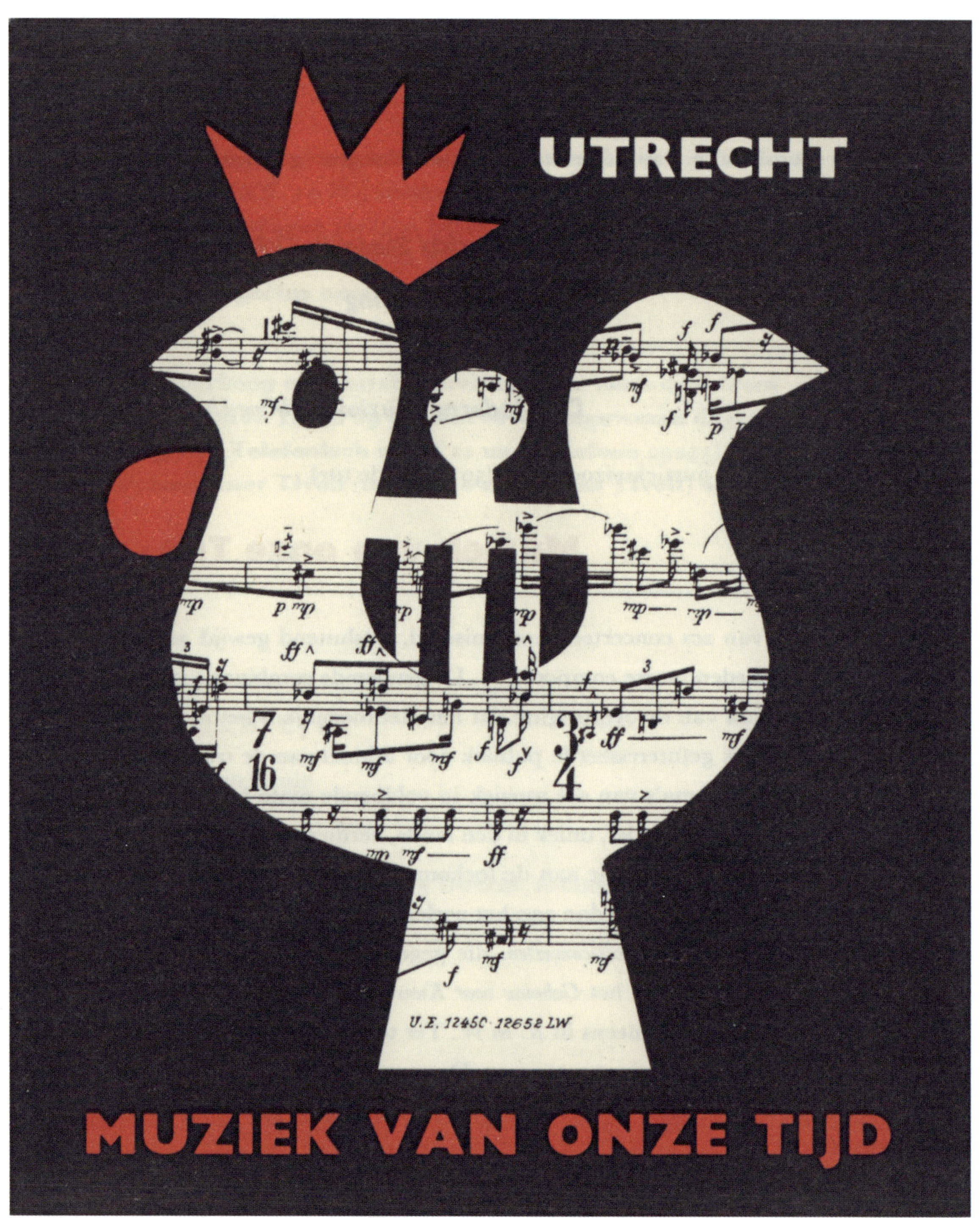
UTRECHT
U.E. 12450·12652 LW
MUZIEK VAN ONZE TIJD

150 JAAR GENOOTSCHAP KUNSTLIEFDE
beitel
en palet
dick
TENTOONSTELLING CENTRAAL MUSEUM UTRECHT
19 OKTOBER – 15 DECEMBER 1957

A new beginning and...

In the early fifties two events would change Bruna's life
forever. He visited the newly opened Matisse Chapel of
the Rosary, and he met the girl next door, Irene de Jongh.
Chris Leeflang, the director of the Broese booksellers where
Bruna had worked, had become a friend and they went on
two painting holidays together to the South of France. They
travelled along the coast taking in as much modern art
and architecture as possible, including Le Corbusier's new
apartment blocks in Marseille, experiencing the Provençal
worlds of Raoul Dufy, Paul Cézanne, Pablo Picasso (in
Vallauris from 1948) and Marc Chagall, who had moved
south from Paris in 1949 to Vence, a few miles west of Nice,
close to the home of Matisse.

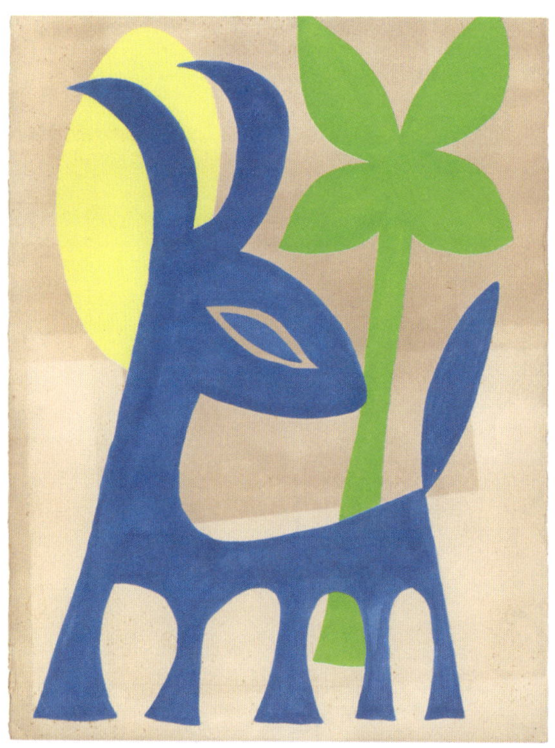

ABOVE
Matisse-inspired painting in
poster paint

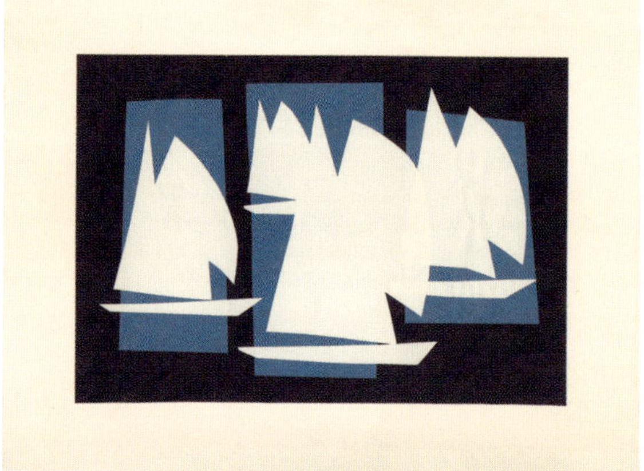

ABOVE
Matisse-inspired collage

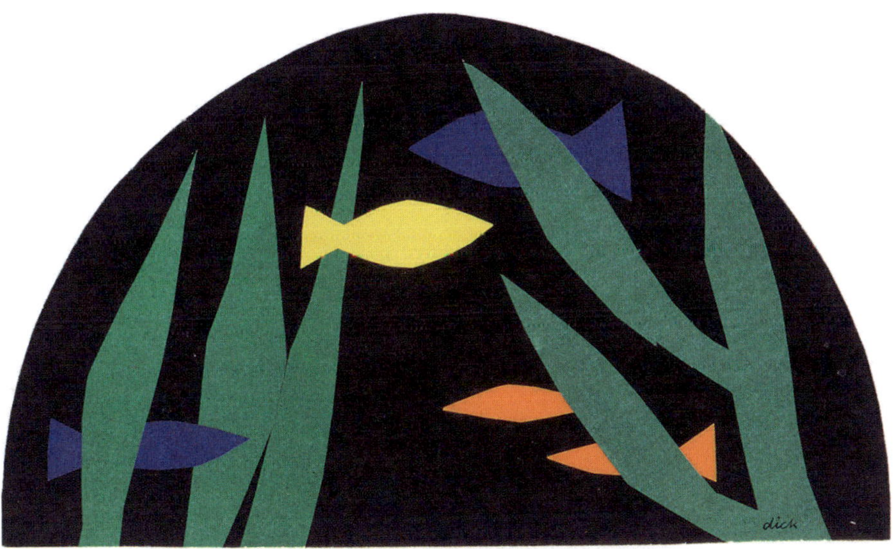

ABOVE
Mural design for the cellar of
De Engelenzang artists' society,
Utrecht, 1957

Matisse had taken on the design of the small chapel in
Vence for a community of Dominicans, commencing in 1948
and taking three years to complete. He created the stained-
glass windows, the campanile, the interior murals, the blue
and white roof pattern, the crucifix and candlesticks, the
confessional door, three holy water fonts and the priest's
chasubles. Discovering Matisse's work in Paris was one
thing; this was a revelation. Matisse himself had considered
the chapel 'his masterpiece'; he had created much of it
using his 'system' of paper cut-outs, 'one of the most
radical inventions of any artist of the 20th century'.[14]

Significantly, when Bruna visited, Matisse's presence was
still palpable, since the artist had barely left the building.
From that first moment, it became Bruna's ultimate aim
to emulate the chapel's purity and beauty in everything he
produced throughout his life. Matisse had honed his art
to its very essence and he would attempt to do the same.
Equally significant for Bruna was Matisse's colour choice
for the stained glass. 'I am looking for something that is
perilous,' Matisse said. 'I almost want it to grate.' His desire,
he said, was that the colours in the chapel would impact on
the visitor, 'like a sharp blow on a gong'.[15]

This is certainly the effect it had on Bruna.

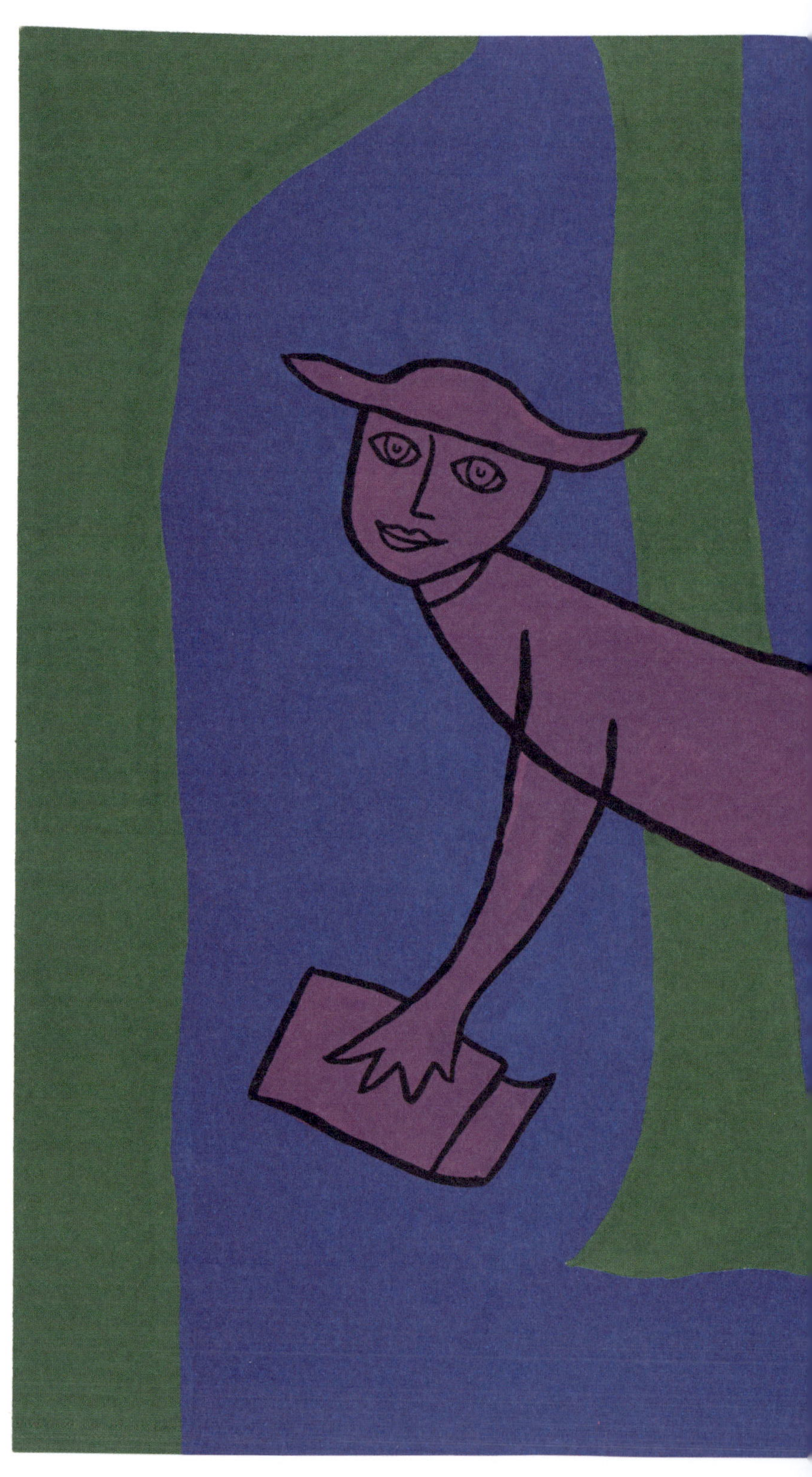

RIGHT
Painting, February 1954

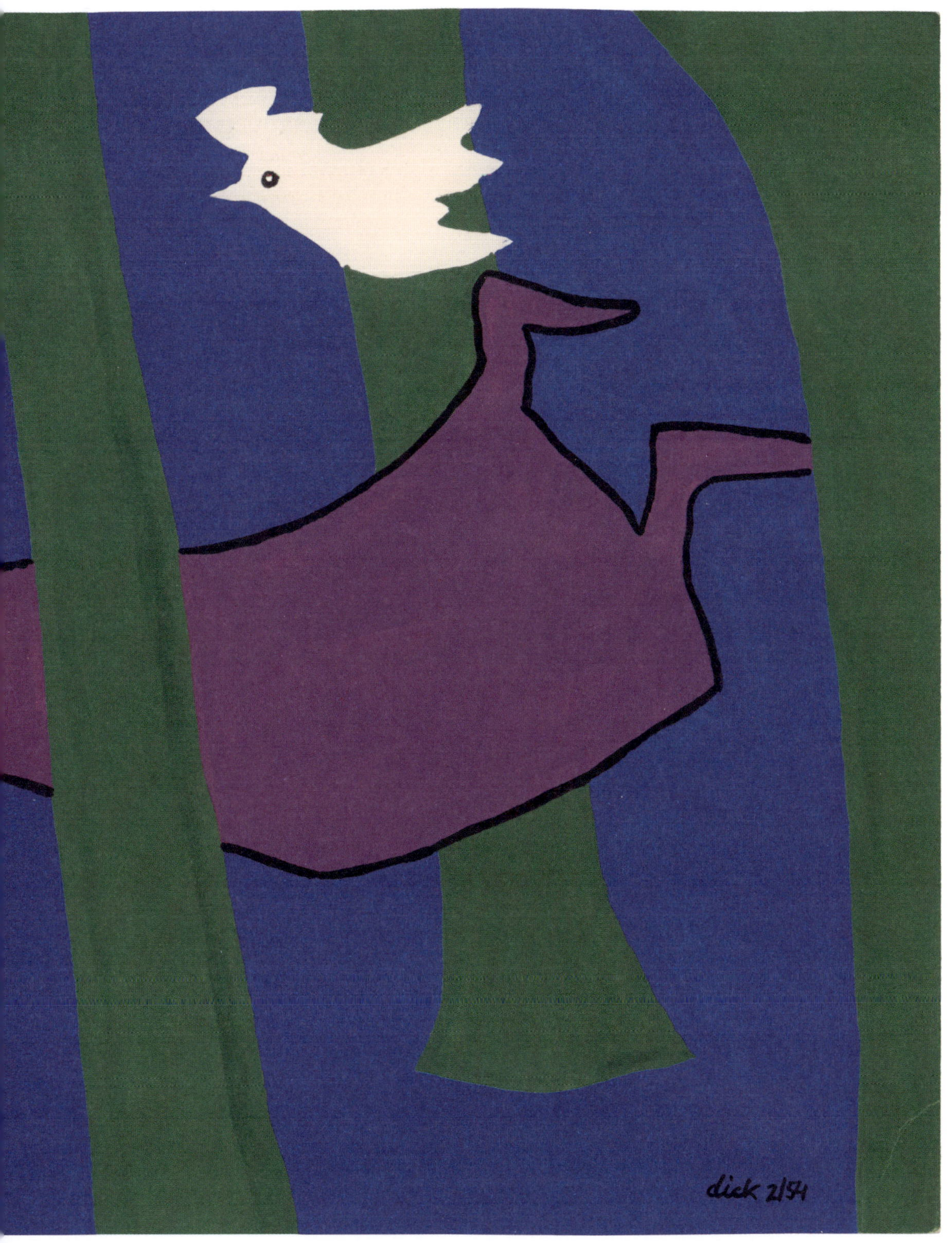

dick 2/54

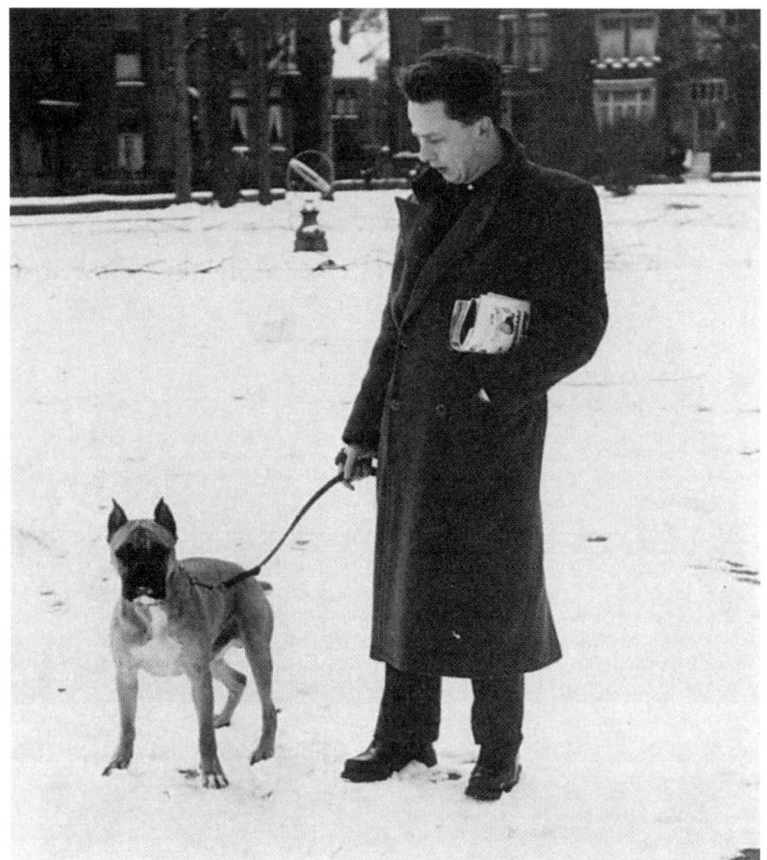

...A happy ending

By 1951 the Bruna family had moved back to Utrecht. Irene de Jongh, six years younger than Bruna, lived across the road. Immediately besotted, he bought a dog, a boxer he named Bruun, so that he could meet Irene out walking her dog. He set up his easel on his parents' balcony to impress her. It seemed to work; all went well enough to embolden Bruna to ask Irene to marry him a year after their meeting. She said no. Heartbroken, Bruna fled to the South of France; if he couldn't have Irene, he would concentrate only on his desire to become a painter. He went to stay with the writers Havank (Hendrikus Frederikus van der Kallen) and Ab Visser, who were holidaying together in Haut-de-Cagnes, with a plan to move to the town of Bandol. But Bruna was too distraught and lovesick to settle. How could he live

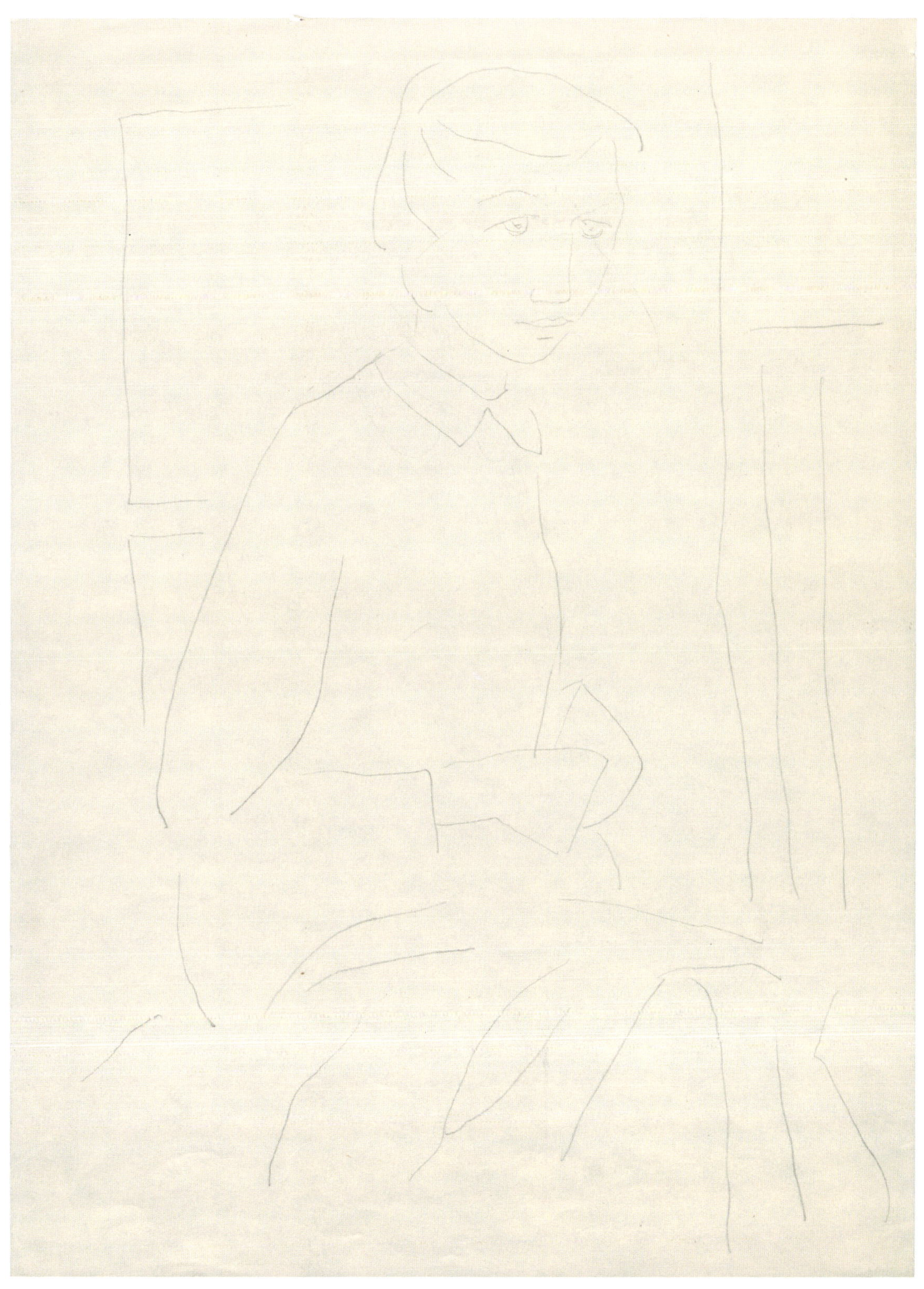

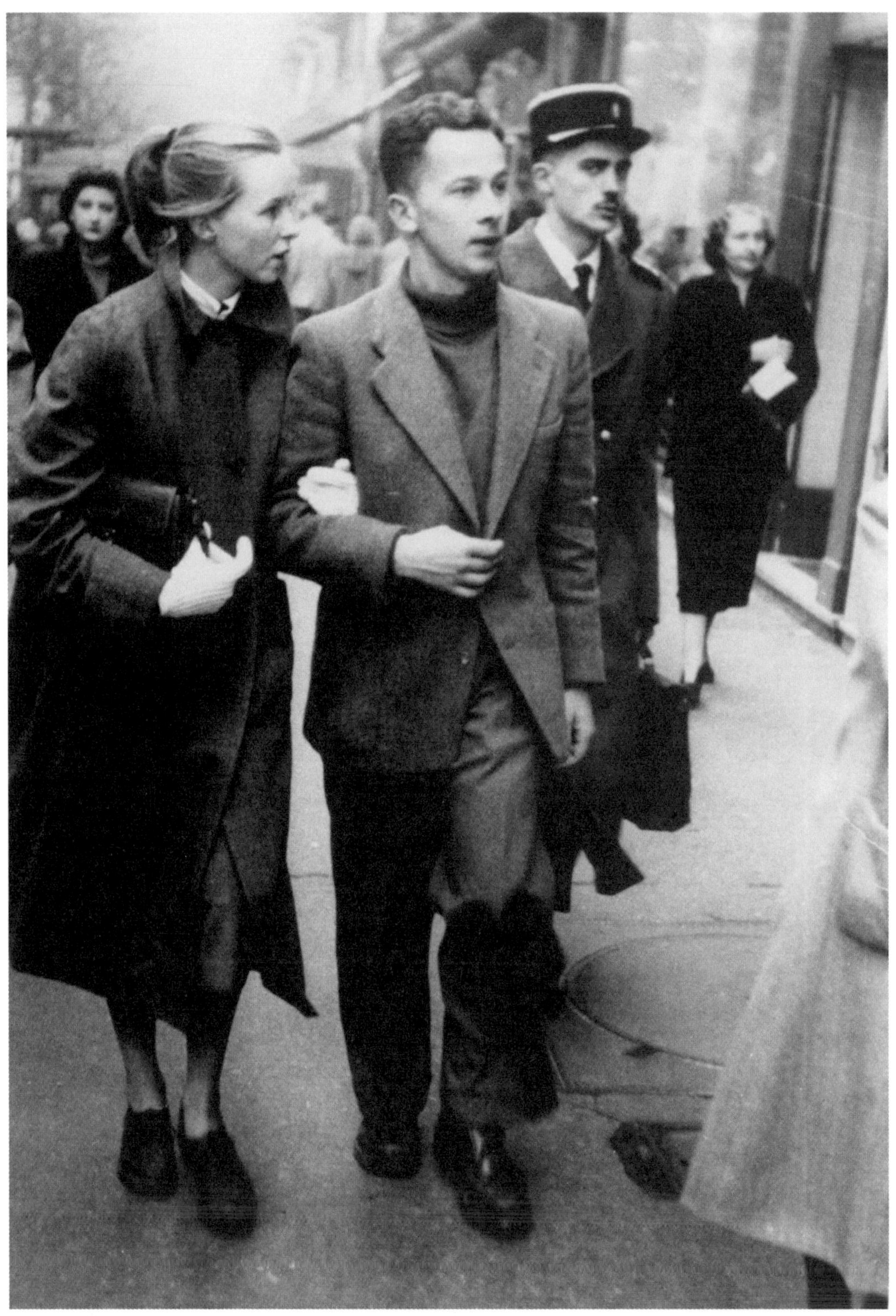

UTRECHT, 14 Juli 1952

L.S.

Wij hebben het genoegen U mede te delen dat
wij met ingang van 15 Juli 1952 aan de Heer
H. M. BRUNA Jr. procuratie hebben verleend.

Directie

A. W. BRUNA & ZOON'S UITG. MIJ. N.V.

De Heer H. M. Bruna zal tekenen:

OPPOSITE

Irene and Dick in Paris,
autumn 1953

ABOVE

The official letter from A. W.
Bruna & Zoon announcing Bruna's
appointment to the company in
July 1952

anywhere without Irene? How could he paint anything?
Within days he raced back to Utrecht and proposed again.
This time Irene accepted and they were married in 1953.

But the marriage came with a condition: Irene's father
insisted that Bruna provide his daughter with the security
of a permanent job. In doing so, he achieved what Bruna's
own father had not been able to accomplish: to compel
Bruna to work full time in the family company. 'So, then
I became a cover designer for A. W. Bruna, my father's
publishing house. That fell into my lap of course.'[16]

RIGHT
Honeymoon scrapbook,
France, 1953

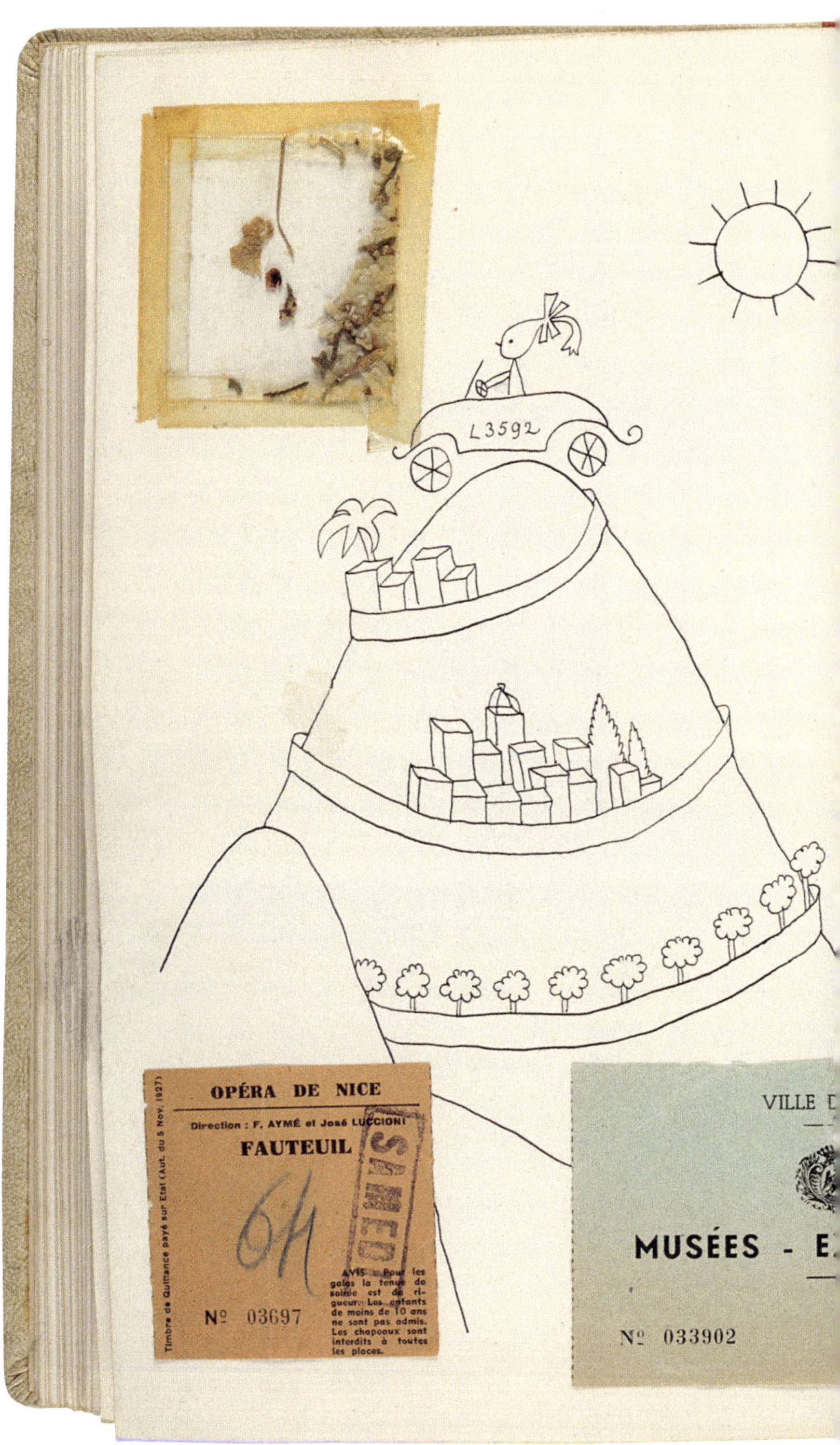
L3592
OPÉRA DE NICE
Direction : F. AYMÉ et José LUCCIONI
FAUTEUIL
64
Nº 03697
Timbre de Quittance payé sur Etat (Aut. du 5 Nov. 1927)
AVIS — Pour les galas la tenue de soirée est de rigueur. Les enfants de moins de 10 ans ne sont pas admis. Les chapeaux sont interdits à toutes les places.
VILLE D
MUSÉES - E
Nº 033902

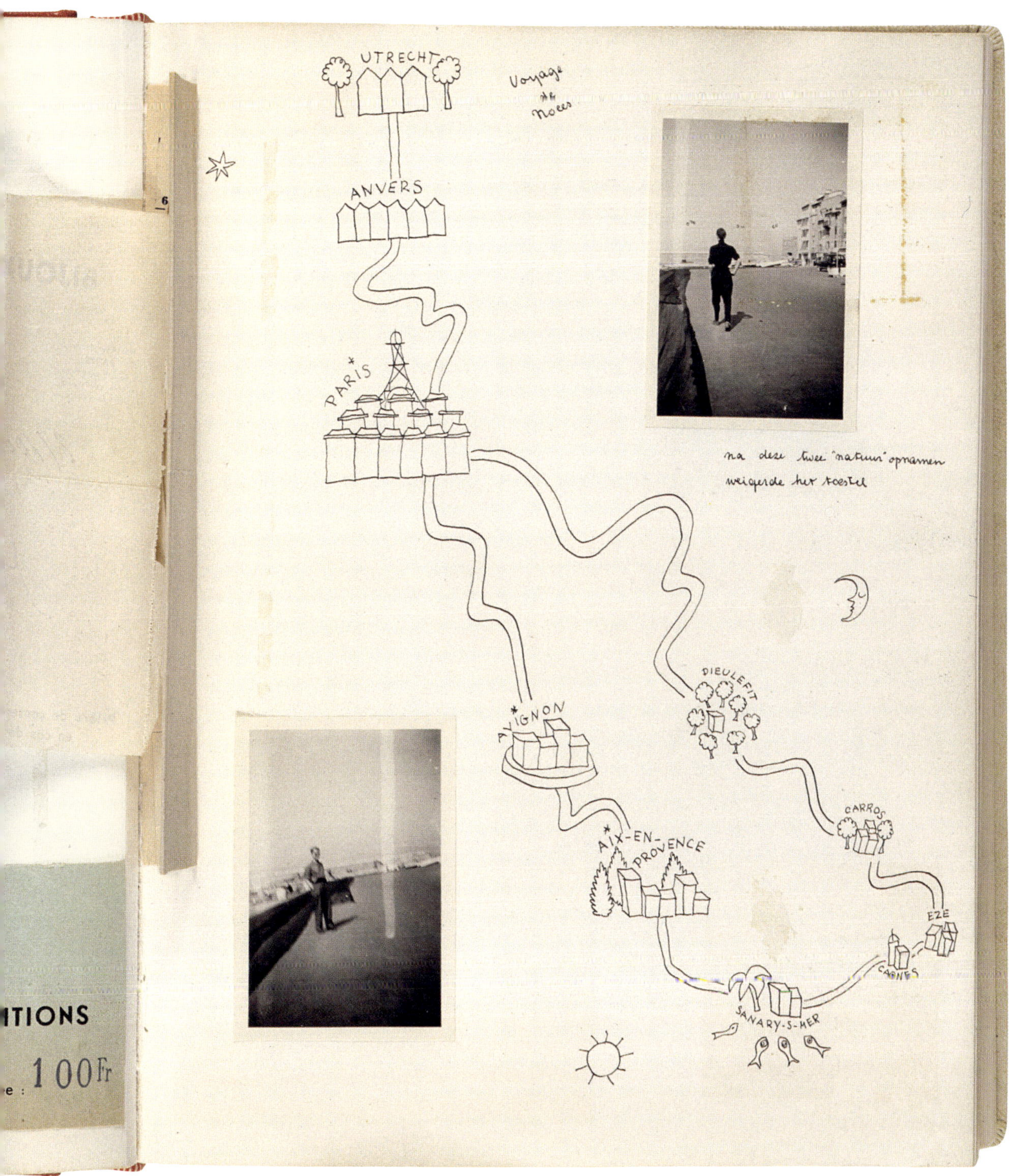

na deze twee "natuur" opnamen
weigerde het toestel

Emerging artist

When Bruna agreed to take a permanent job at A. W. Bruna
in 1952, he assumed his dream of being an artist really was
dead. In reality, working as a full-time designer allowed him
to experiment creatively while providing stability for himself
and Irene. This would prove to be the most productive
decade of his life. And, in Irene, he had gained a cheerleader
and, more importantly, his very own 'chief critic'.[17] From
here on, nothing went through without her approval.

As Irene said, 'He had a lot of pluck, because he did a lot
of different things. Sometimes he took risks…without the
book covers he would never have been able to develop his
own graphic style.'[18] And in time, Bruna himself would
come to acknowledge that his graphic design years were
'my art school'.

Bruna's drawings from 1953 show how his approach
was changing. He began to sketch not what he saw but how
objects related to each other; how they worked with and
against each other to create an atmosphere. Objects are

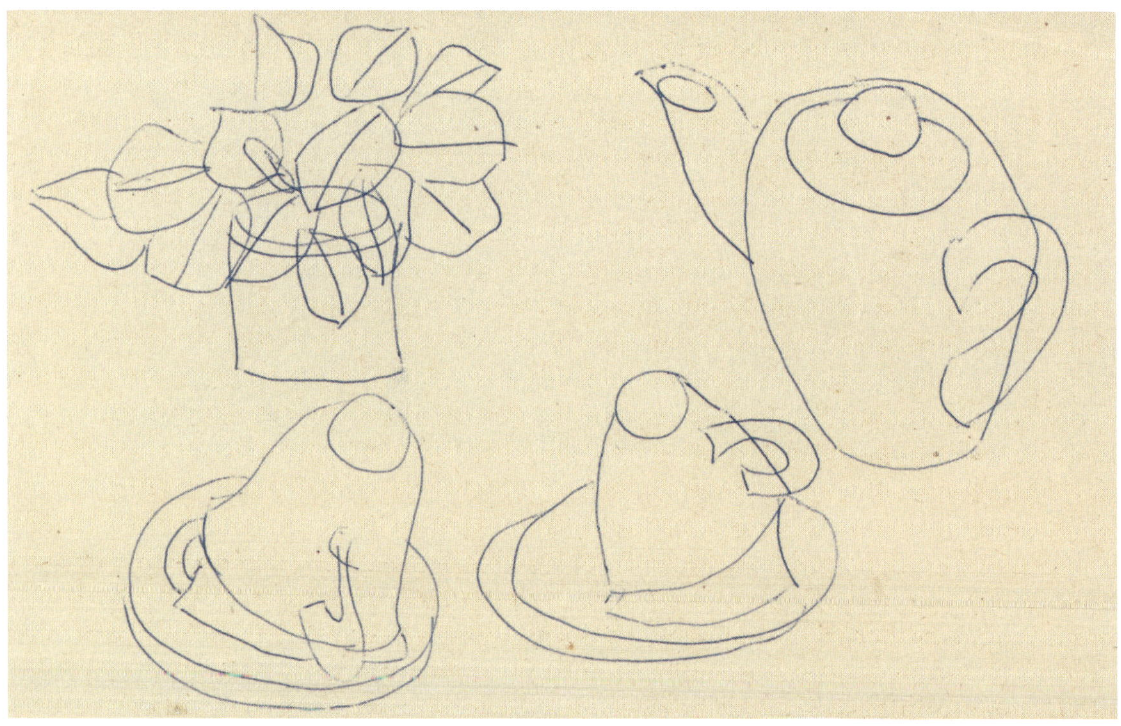

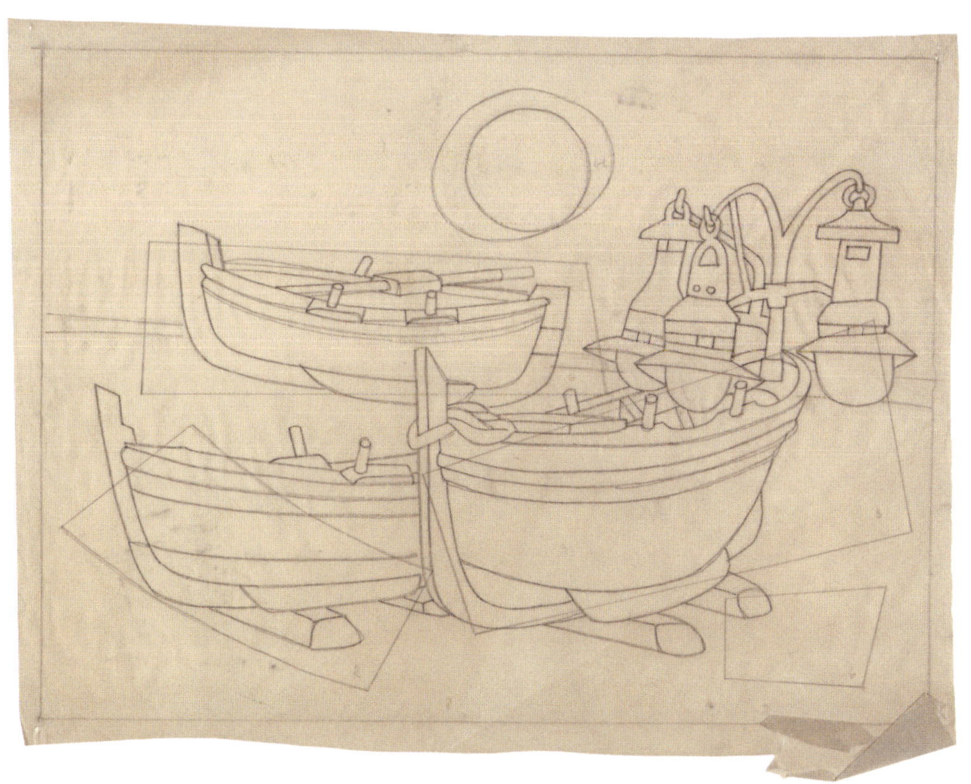

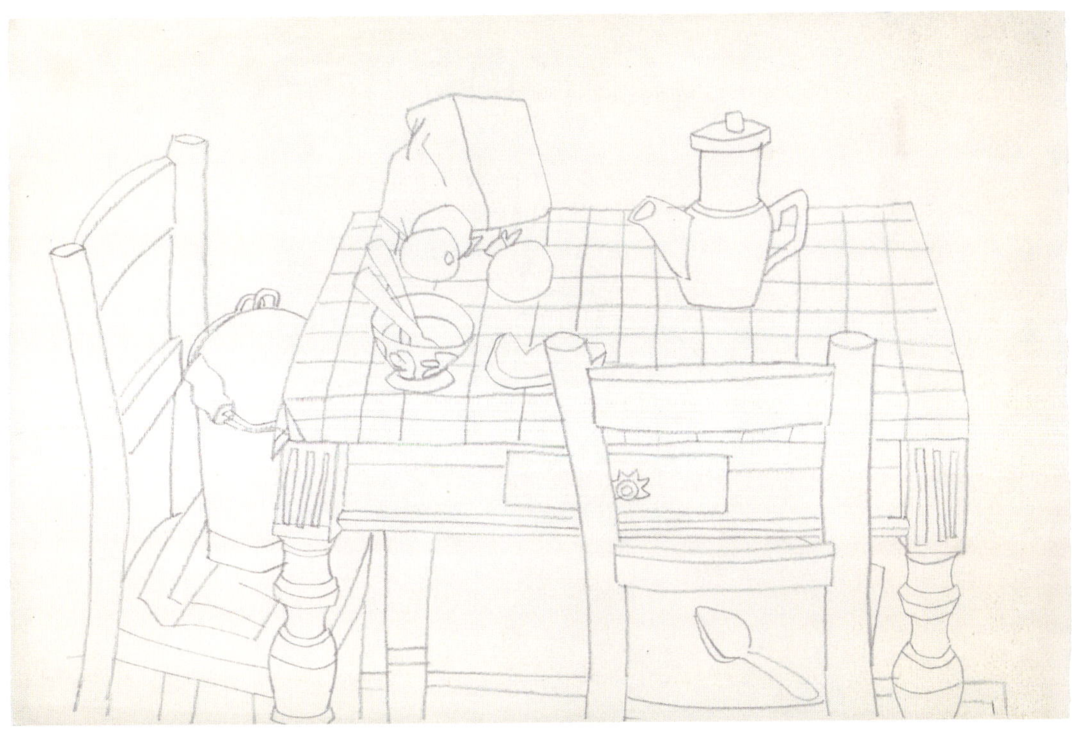

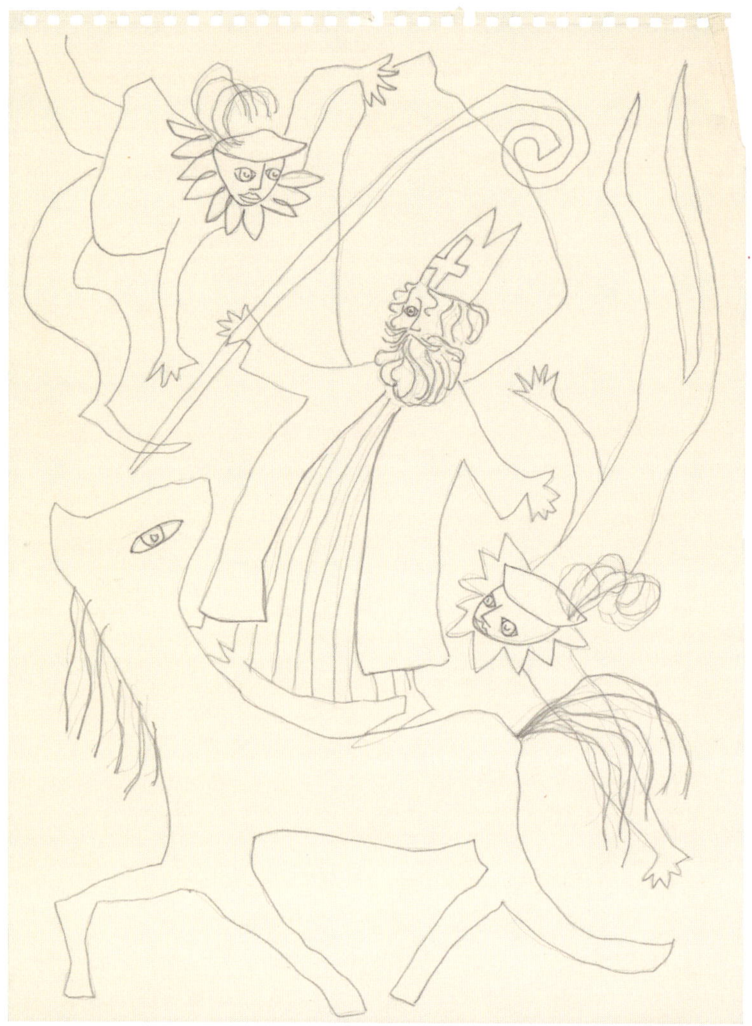

often isolated from their setting. This is evident from the
honeymoon drawings and subsequent holidays with Irene
in the South of France, Spain and Italy. He drew for
pleasure, he drew to experiment, he drew for possible
future reference; he simply drew and drew. The drawings
became less self-conscious and studied, more relaxed and
fun. He started taking photographs for reference, picking
out interesting objects that created an atmosphere worth
replicating. He cut out images of objects from newspapers;
he was always on the lookout, always the artist.

The influence of his heroes is still clear to see in these

Unpublished drawing of
Sinterklaas (Saint Nicholas), 1954

drawings but Bruna's personality shines through. Referring to the work of Léger, which was so important in this development, Bruna explained:

> *For the first time, I saw perspective disappearing in favour of construction and colours becoming flat so there was no transition any more. I remember at the time when I saw those clear forms…with those iron constructions, I started drawing nuts and bolts and sockets and things like that, things with very clear outlines.*[19]

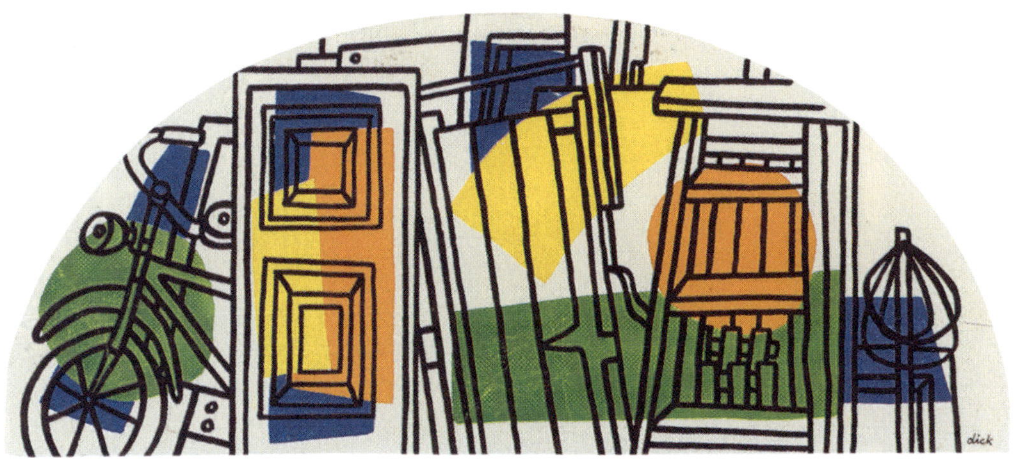

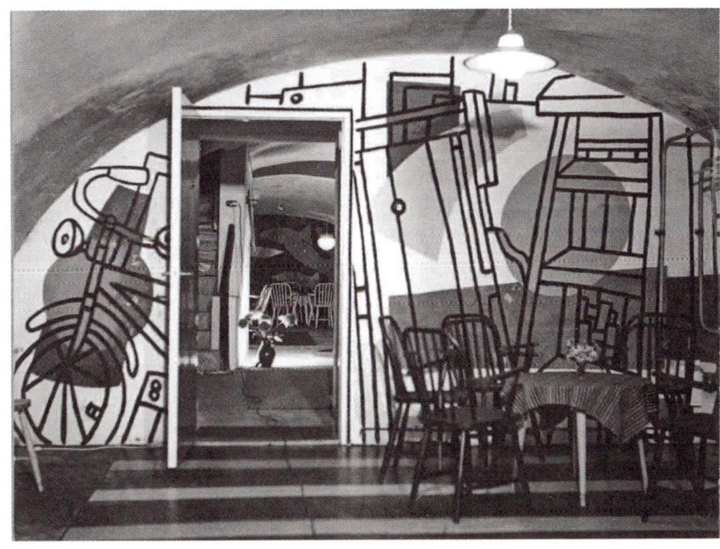

ABOVE AND RIGHT
Design and finished mural for the cellar of De Engelenzang artists' society, Utrecht, 1957, showing the influence of Léger

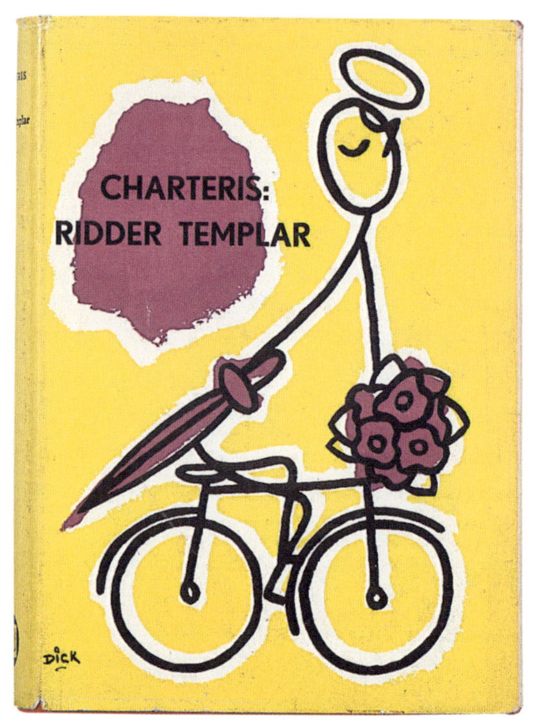
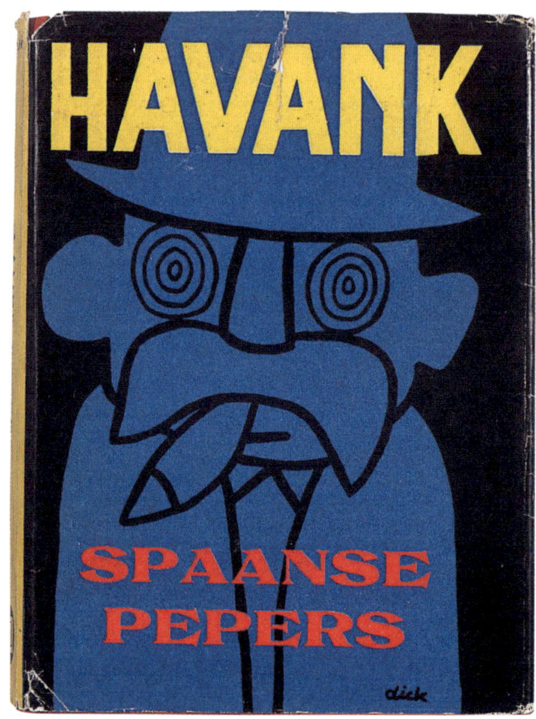

Publishing

As Bruna's style was changing, so too was the publishing industry. The postwar years marked a revolution in the paperback book market throughout the world. The branded paperback, famously invented in 1934 when Penguin Books founder, Allen Lane, got stranded at a train station with nothing to read and very little from which to choose, would have been familiar to Bruna. His stint working in London coincided with Jan Tschichold's redesign of the Penguin logo.

In the Netherlands, publishers were looking for a way out of the wartime doldrums now that paper shortages and prices were easing. As the fifties progressed, utilitarianism gave way to optimism and increased investment; quality was added to low-priced quantity with better paper and colour printing. Rival publishers in the Netherlands had already launched series fiction in the early fifties: the Salamanders from Querido and the Prismas from the Utrecht-based Het Spectrum.

Two early book covers: Leslie Charteris, *Ridder Templar* (*Knight Templar*), 1952, and Havank, *Spaanse Pepers* ('Spanish peppers'), design for a Book of the Month cover, 1954

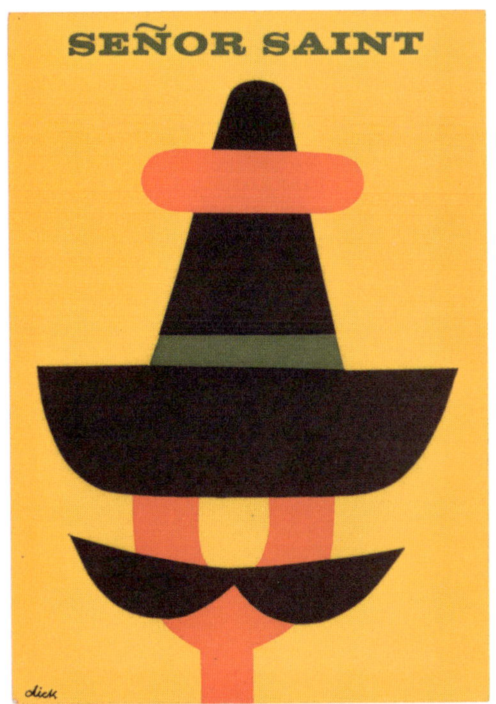

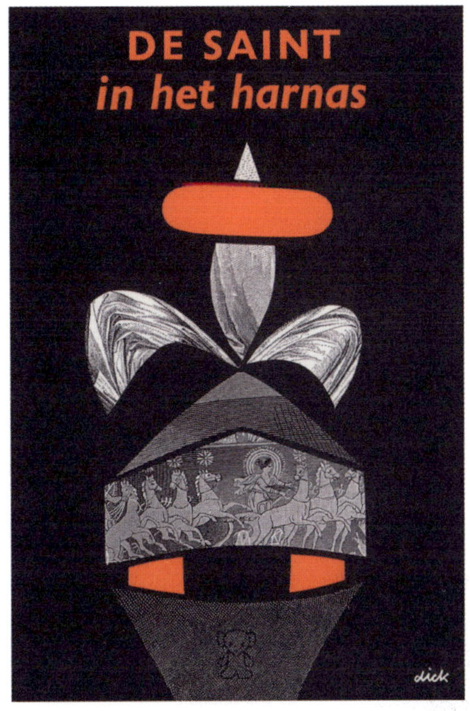

ABOVE

Covers for two Leslie Charteris books: *Señor Saint*, 1962, and *De Saint in het harnas* (*Saint Errant*), 1963

At A. W. Bruna, a branded series of crime fiction was conceived in the autumn of 1954. As detective stories in particular were gaining market traction, this was an obvious route.

Bruna would have seen how American crime fiction was à la mode in Paris and piled high on the stalls of the bouquinistes along the Seine. Abs Bruna already published several successful fictional detectives including Georges Simenon's Maigret, Leslie Charteris's The Saint and, Dutch favourite, Havank's De Schaduw (The Shadow) through the 'book of the month' series launched in the immediate postwar period. This provided a strong backlist from which to select, launch and build.

A. W. Bruna had two further advantages: the triumvirate of commercial director Abs Bruna, publisher Jaap Romijn and designer Bruna, and the facility to distribute and sell their own books through the station kiosks, where their target readers were to be found. Abs Bruna didn't read

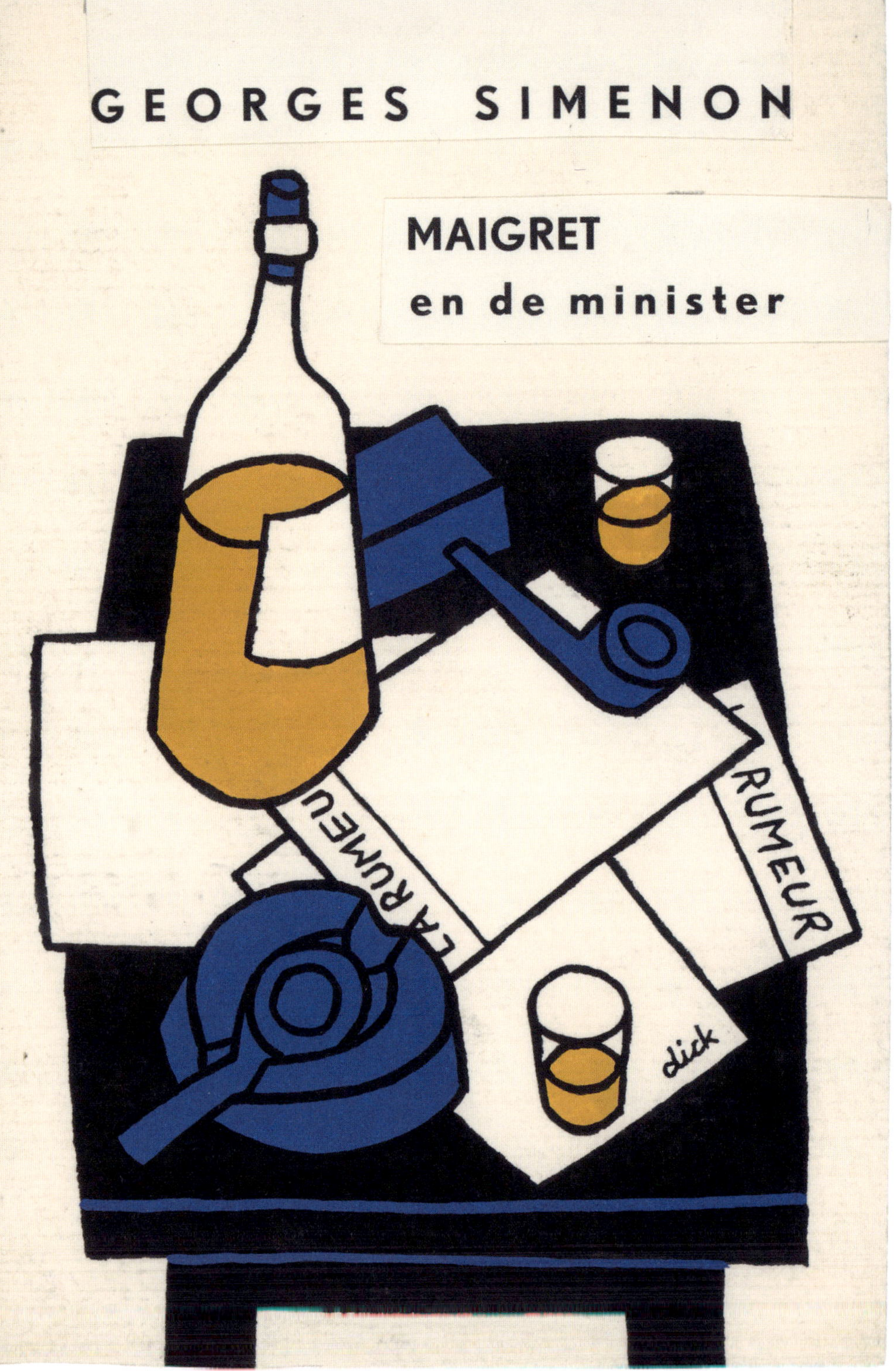

GEORGES SIMENON
MAIGRET
en de minister
LA RUMEUR
LA RUMEUR
dick
SIMENON
MAIGRET EN DE MINISTER

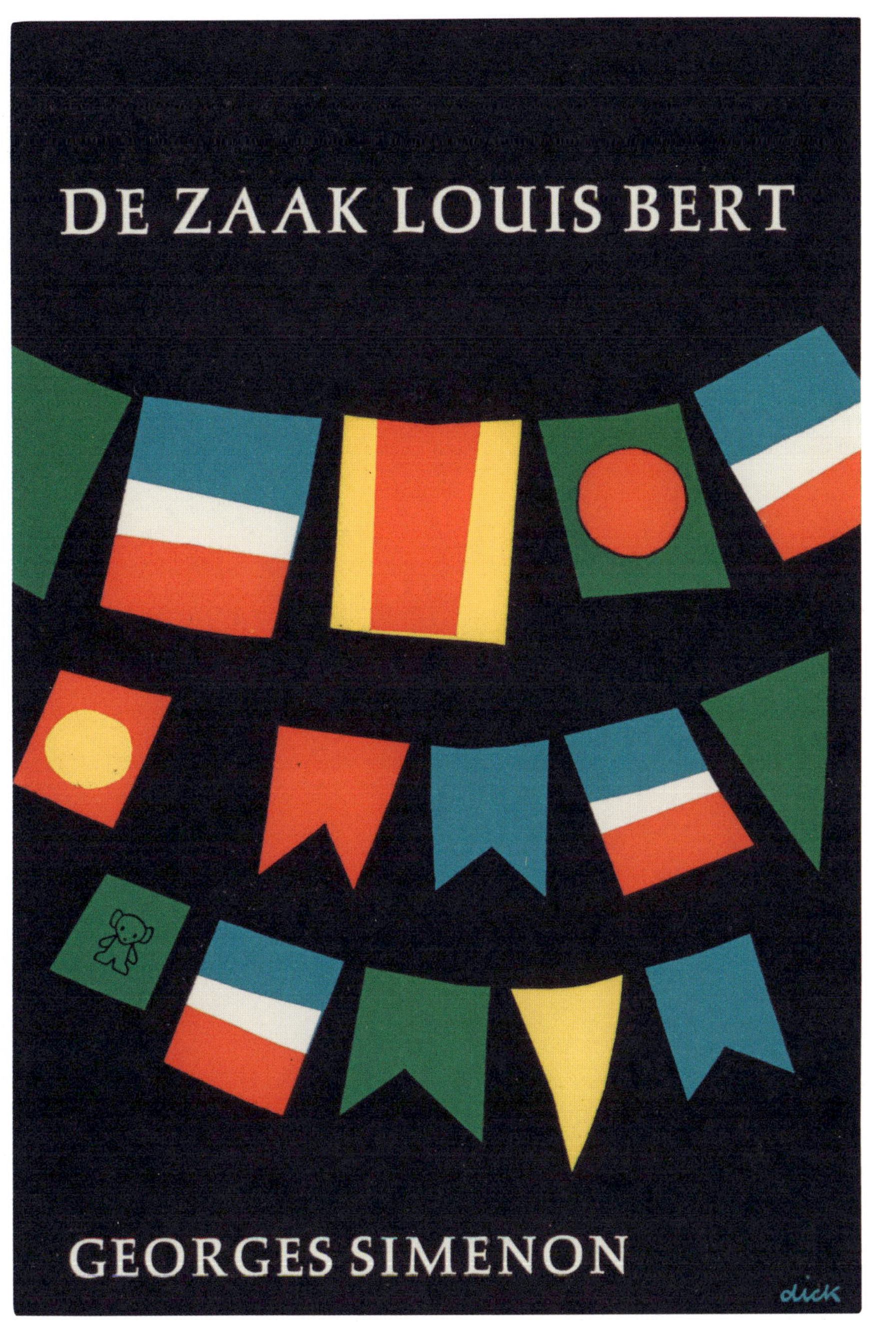

OPPOSITE

Cover design for Georges Simenon,
Maigret en de minister (*Maigret
and the Minister*), 1956

ABOVE

Cover for Georges Simenon,
De zaak Louis Bert ('The case of
Louis Bert'), 1965

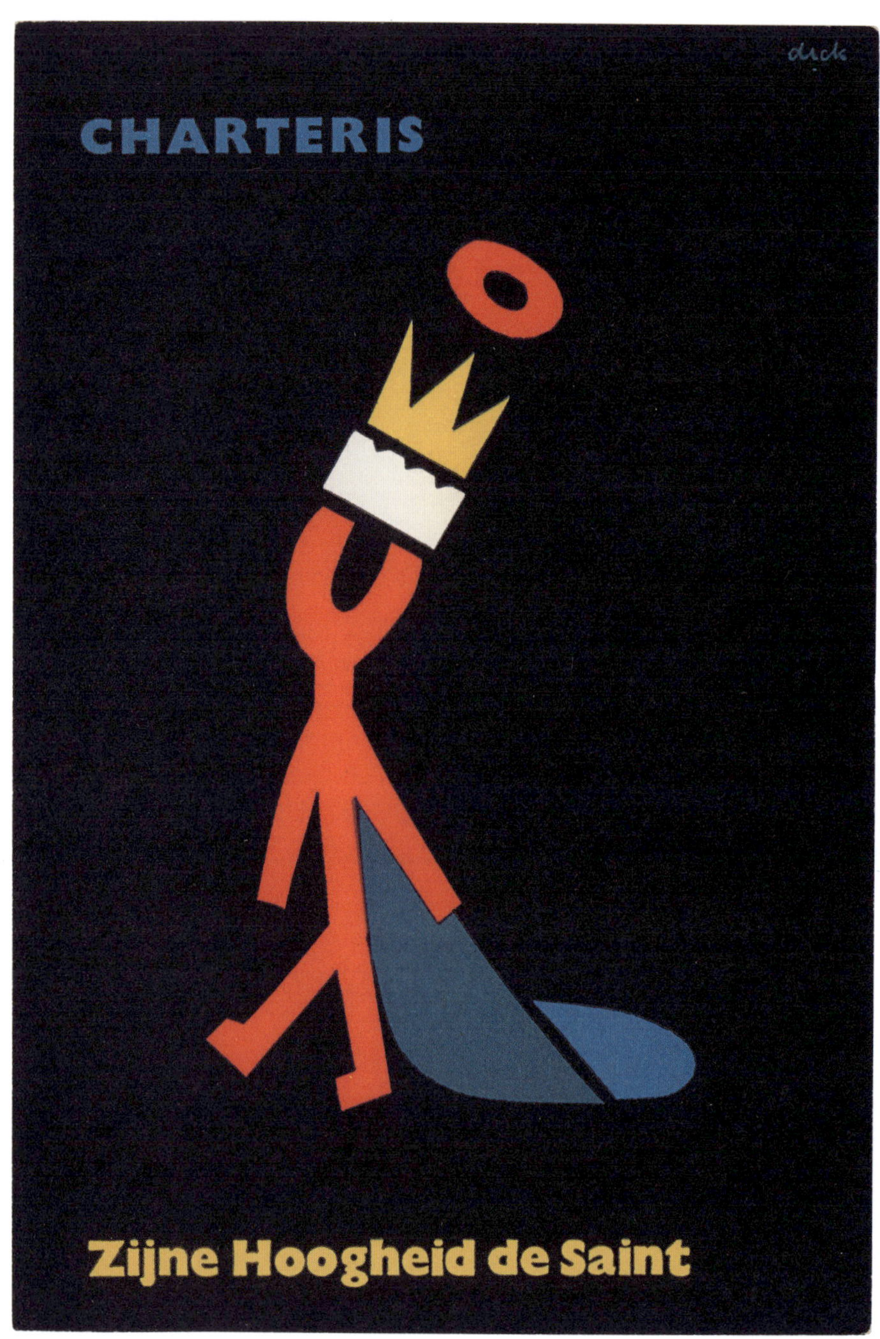

dick
CHARTERIS
Zijne Hoogheid de Saint

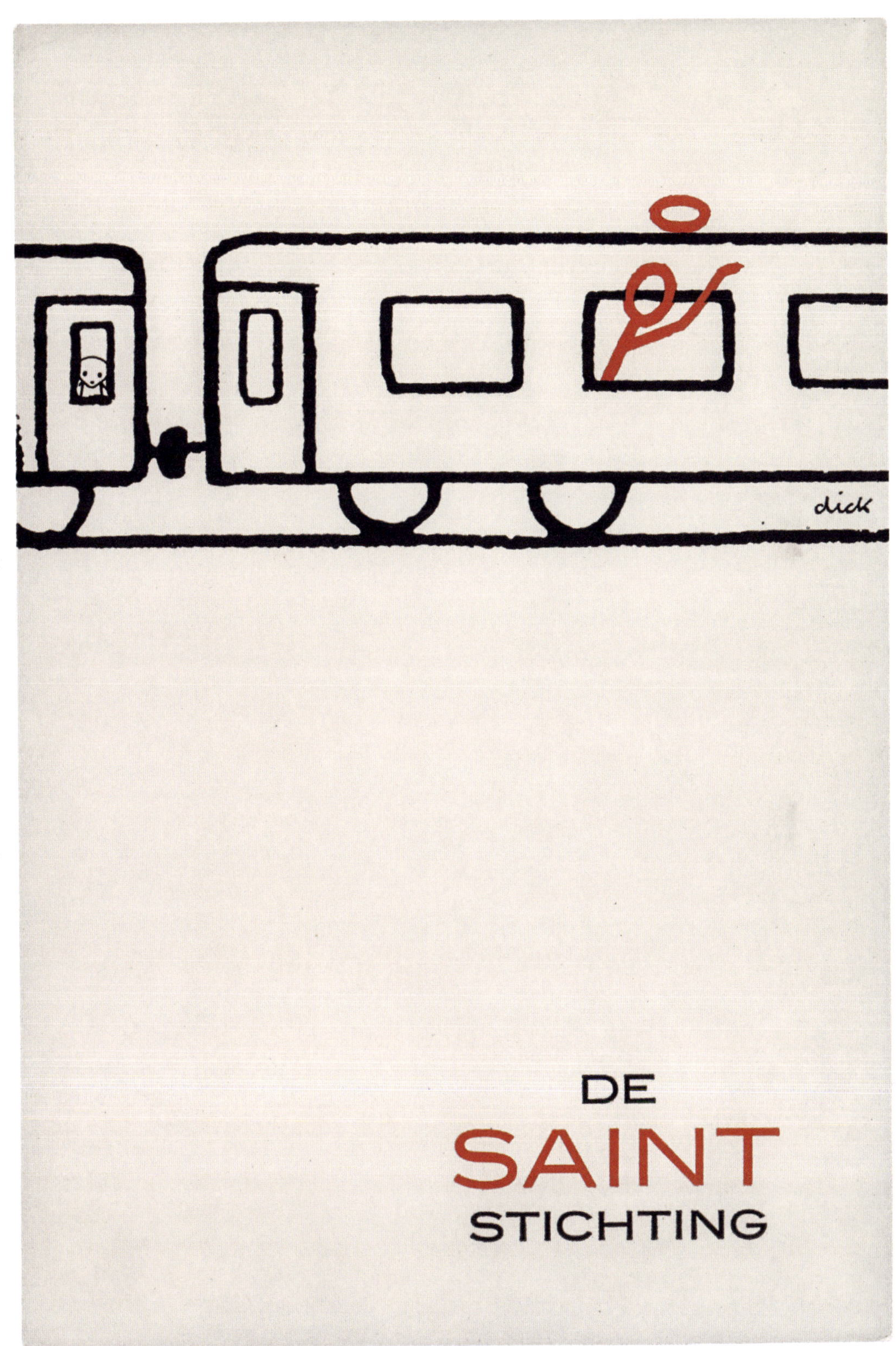

DE
SAINT
STICHTING

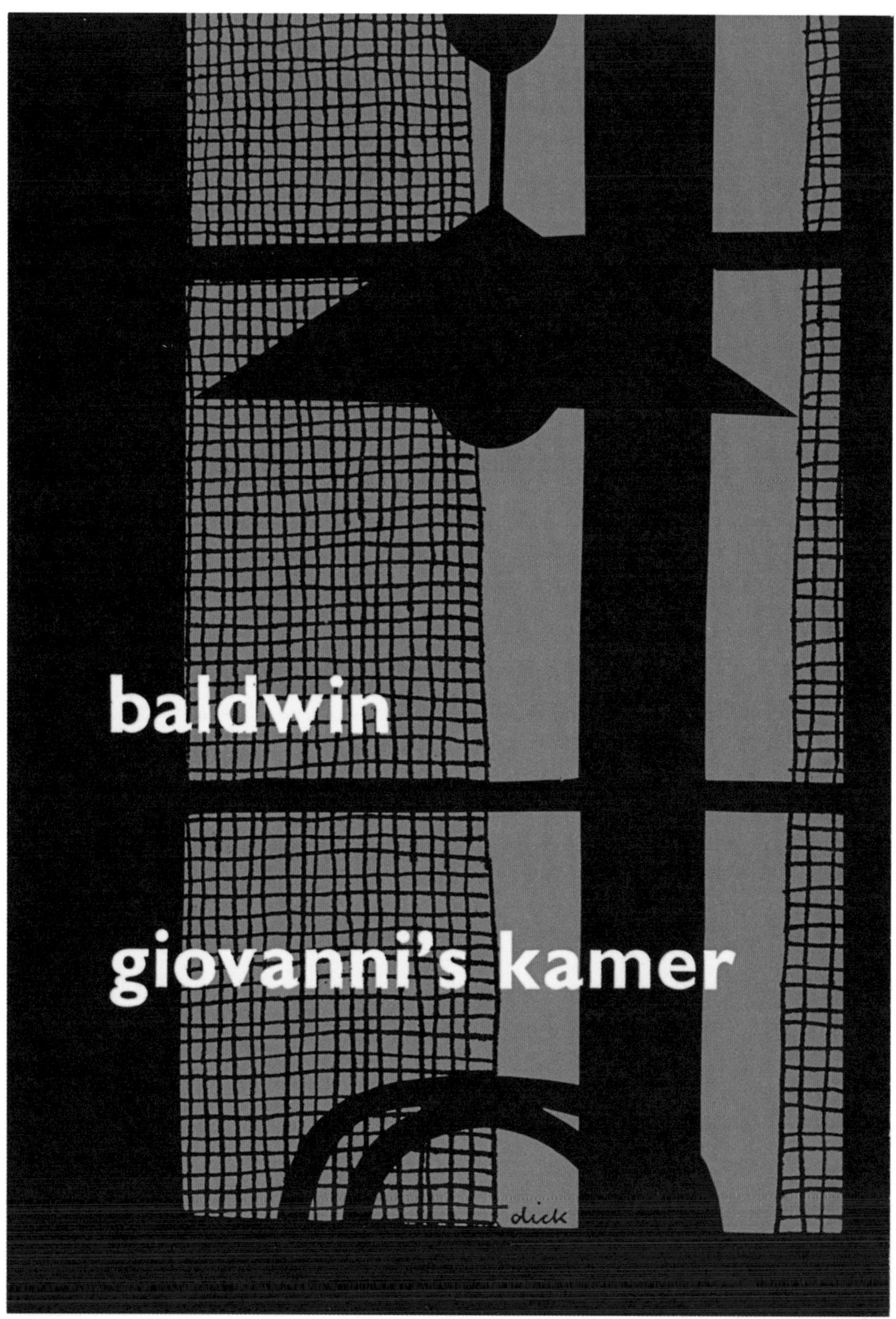

baldwin
giovanni's kamer
dick

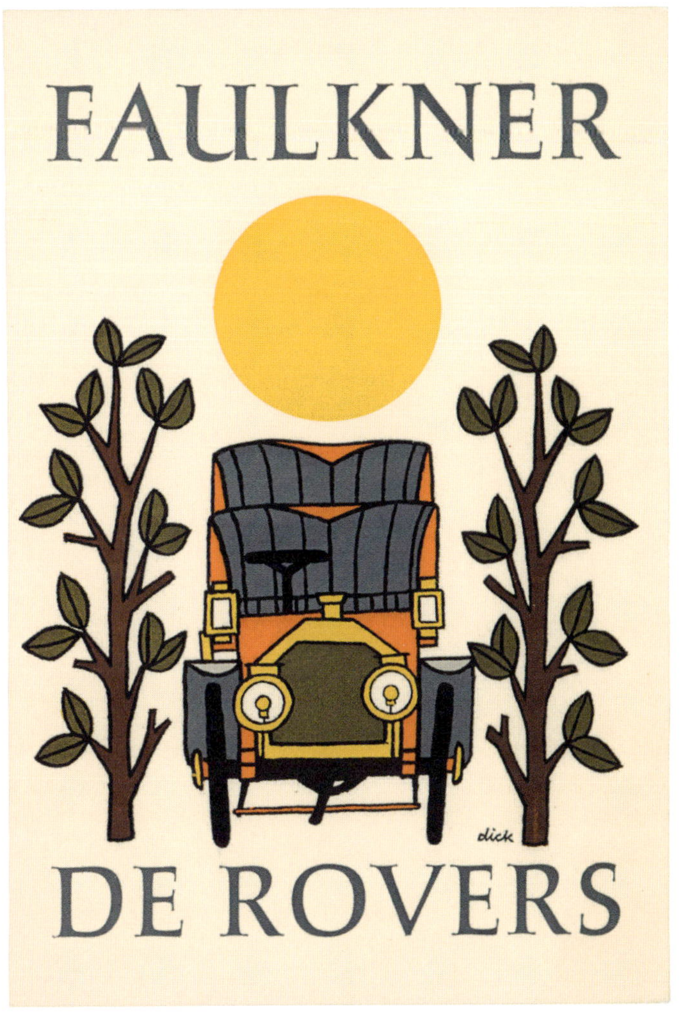

books, not as far as his sons were aware – 'because books are not for reading, but for selling. But he had a good feeling, a *fingerspitzengefühl* [intuition], for what had to be spent and especially for what you shouldn't do,' Bruna explained.[20]

Jaap Romijn bridged the gap between father and son. An artist, editor and publisher, he saw the publishing business from both the financial and aesthetic sides and was a strong supporter of the young Bruna. His literary affiliations led to the creation of the more highbrow *Witte Beertjes* (White Bears) series in the mid-sixties. It was Romijn who insisted on including writers such as Jean-Paul Sartre on the list.[21]

OPPOSITE AND ABOVE

Covers for James Baldwin, *Giovanni's kamer* (*Giovanni's Room*), 1966, and William Faulkner, *De rovers (The Reivers)*, 1963

Bruna may not have understood the financial side of
the business but in relation to the design of the books, he
had his own *fingerspitzengefühl*. He knew the series had to
appeal to people in a hurry, literally. They had to catch the
attention of the traveller, and gain brand recognition.
To achieve this he developed a new style of cover design,
which was about more than simply selling content, it
was about impact, attraction and series identity. Bruna
recognized the power of an immediate visual connection.
He wanted to sound the 'gong' to which Matisse had referred.

The success of the list was dependent on printing and
selling large quantities to keep the prices low and to
maintain the momentum of mass production. This put a
considerable pressure on the designer to deliver the covers.
Undaunted, the usually diffident Bruna set to work.

The Black Bear

First came the bear; a brand needs a logo. This was
relatively straightforward, since a bear had long been
associated with the name Bruna, *bruin* meaning brown,

Original logo design for *Zwarte
Beertjes* (Black Bears), 1955–61

Revised logo design for *Zwarte
Beertjes*, 1962 onwards

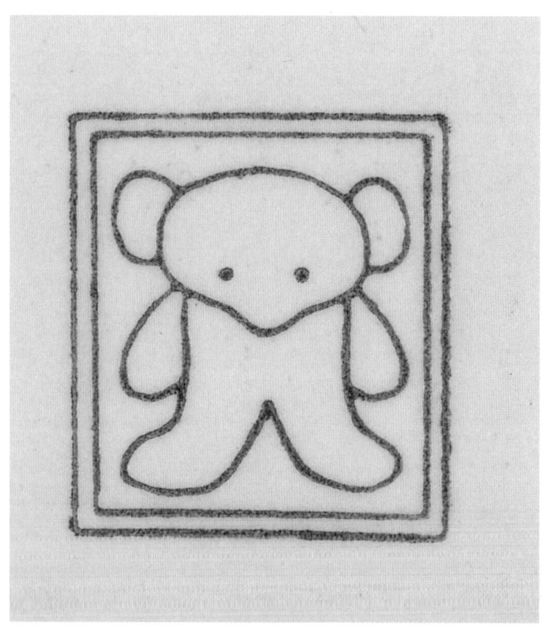

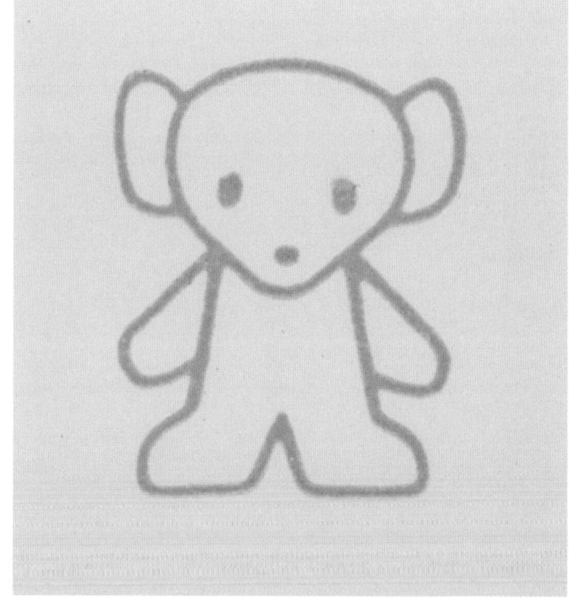

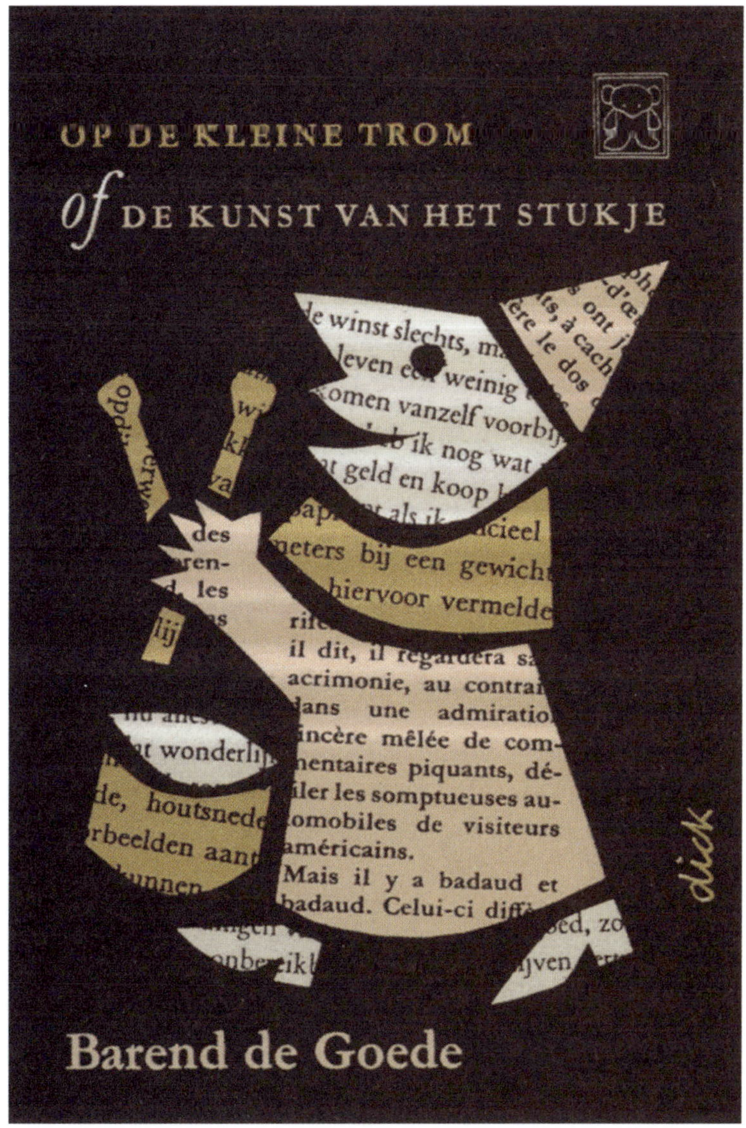

An early book cover design for *Zwarte Beertjes* showing the original logo, 1958

and was already used as a trademark. Bruna made this bear black, to create an element of intrigue and darkness and convey the content of the list. But, because of his fearful disposition, he decided not to make the series look too scary; more mysterious than menacing. This gave the books a broader appeal and enabled the publishers to add non-detective titles to the series once it was established. The first incarnation of the Black Bear logo was framed but quite quickly set free of its box, making it easier to

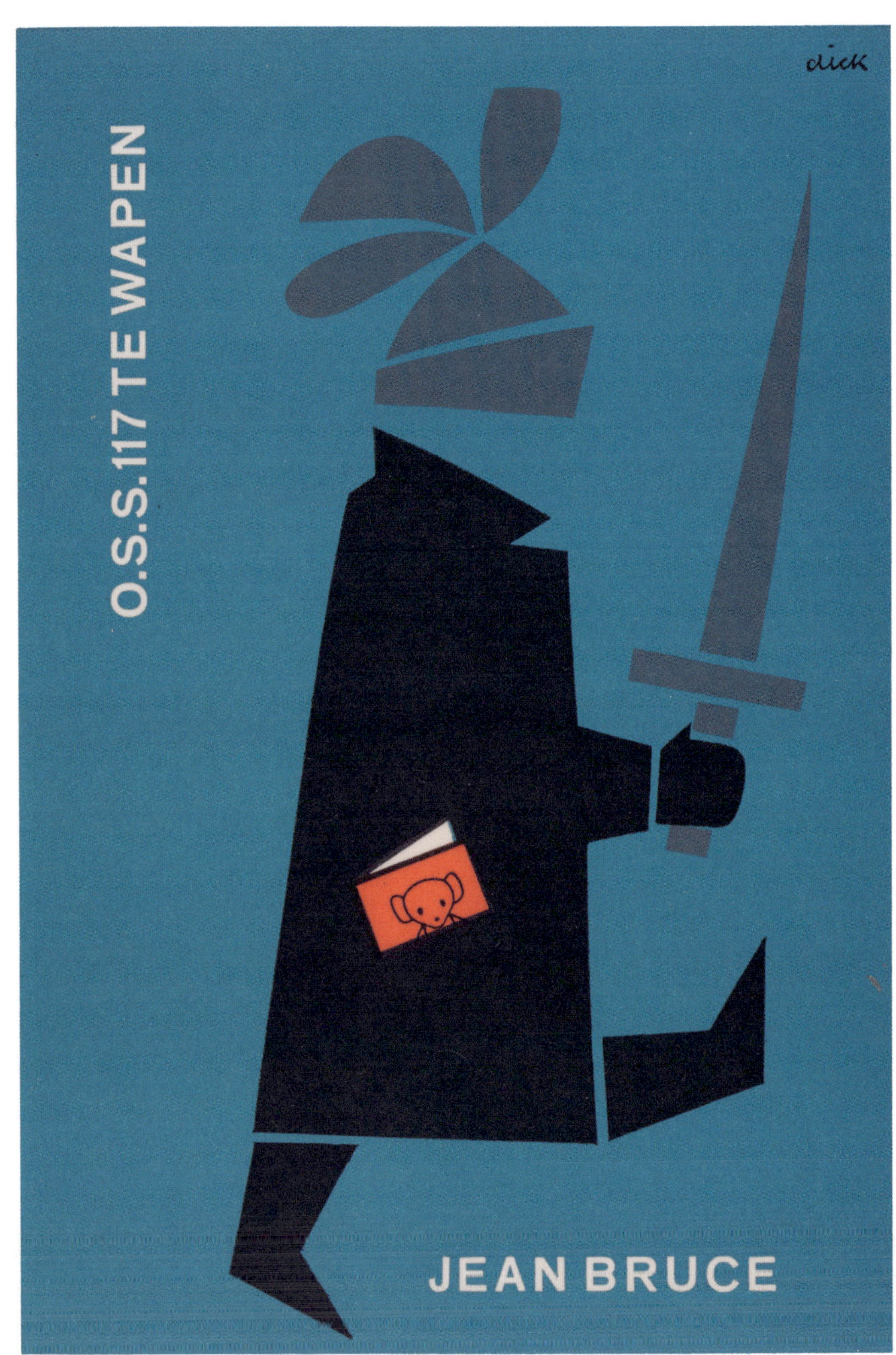

dick
O.S.S.117 TE WAPEN
JEAN BRUCE

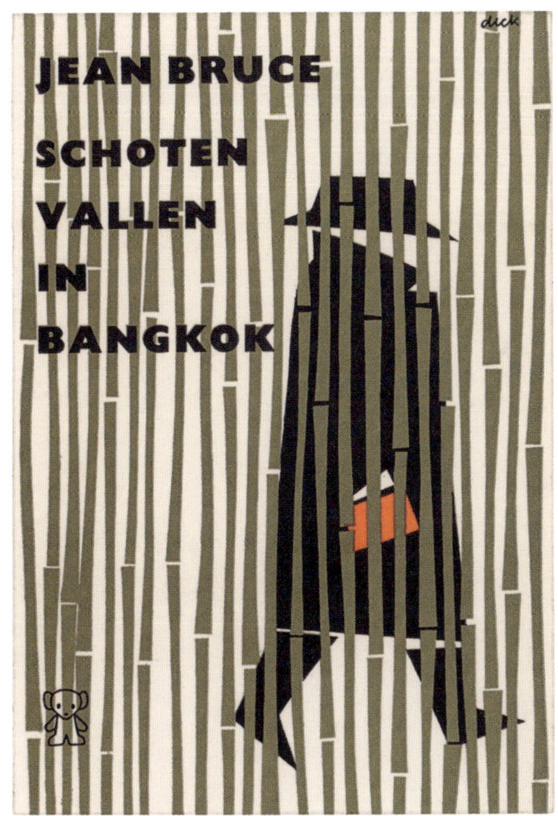

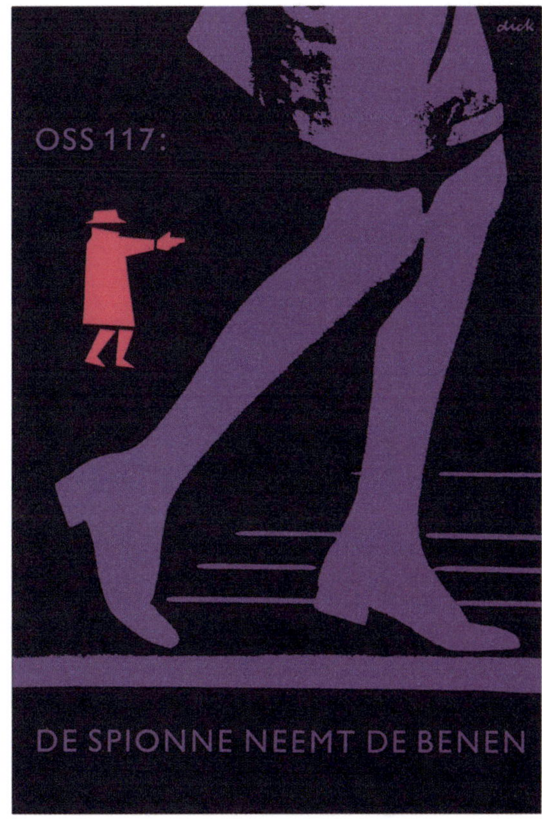

OPPOSITE

Cover for Jean Bruce, *O.S.S.117 te wapen* ('O.S.S.117 at arms'), showing integrated logo, 1966

ABOVE

Covers for Jean Bruce: *Schoten vallen in Bangkok* ('Shots fall in Bangkok'), 1964, and *O.S.S.117: De spionne neemt de benen* ('O.S.S.117: The spy takes off'), 1971

manipulate on the cover design. Occasionally, in playful mood, Bruna made the bear integral to the illustration.

The *Zwarte Beertjes*, the Black Bears, launched in 1955 with six titles, rising to about eighteen in 1956 before catapulting to well over one hundred a year, with Bruna designing every single cover. At first, he had to work in black, for reasons of economy, but as the series grew, expanding beyond crime fiction, so came the colour. There is no sign in his output that he ever felt overwhelmed or jaded by the scale of the work. The covers reveal an illustrator and graphic artist of extraordinary discipline, process and insight. He brought everything he had to the series, his influences, skills, work ethic and, then, his personality; he was a one-man design industry.

Bruna revealed how he worked in an article in the
Belgian press in 1962: firstly, he always read the books,
usually delivered to him in bulk at manuscript stage. There
were no editorial cover briefs to which he could refer. He
wanted to ascertain the atmosphere of the story for himself,
often making sketches as he went along. As he read, he
would begin to see the stories in terms of colour. Or he
might imagine himself in a particular setting, for example
a Simenon story took him back to a drizzly Paris. This
association might bring colour and shapes to mind. The next
stage would be to experiment with different-sized cut-outs
using paint manufacturers' catalogues. 'I'll play around with
these colours – cutting out, pasting and tearing. I attach
much importance to spontaneity and so I do everything
straight away in the chosen colour.'[22]

If he didn't like it, he'd start again, as many times
as he felt necessary. 'I place the forms I've made onto a
background under glass, exactly the same size as the cover,
so no more reducing or enlarging.' Then he would leave that
design, moving on to another one before returning to the
first one to make a final decision, eliminating elements until
it was as simple as possible. When he was satisfied that
the covers were ready, he would bring them to the printers
himself to see them on press.

The *Zwarte Beertjes*' covers were designed without a
grid with no regularity in positioning of title or author
name; objects floating on a plane came together to form an
arresting image, yet they looked like a series with Bruna's
inimitable 'illustration' style. 'I realized at that rate I
could and must use every technique available – drawing,
tearing, collage, everything.'[23] As with his children's books,
Bruna had no desire to experiment with typefaces. He felt
unqualified to do so and he didn't want the lettering to
interfere with the design.

One of the most distinguishing features of the covers
was the use of motifs and silhouettes to link books within
the series. For instance, in the Maigret stories by Simenon,
there is always a pipe, for Charteris's The Saint, a graphic
halo. Much to Bruna's delight, on a visit to the office,
Rietveld pointed at the cover of *The Pirate Saint* and said,
'Young man, that is a really beautiful little shape.'[24]

Cover for Georges Simenon,
Maigret en de onbekende wreker
('Maigret and the unknown
avenger'), 1964

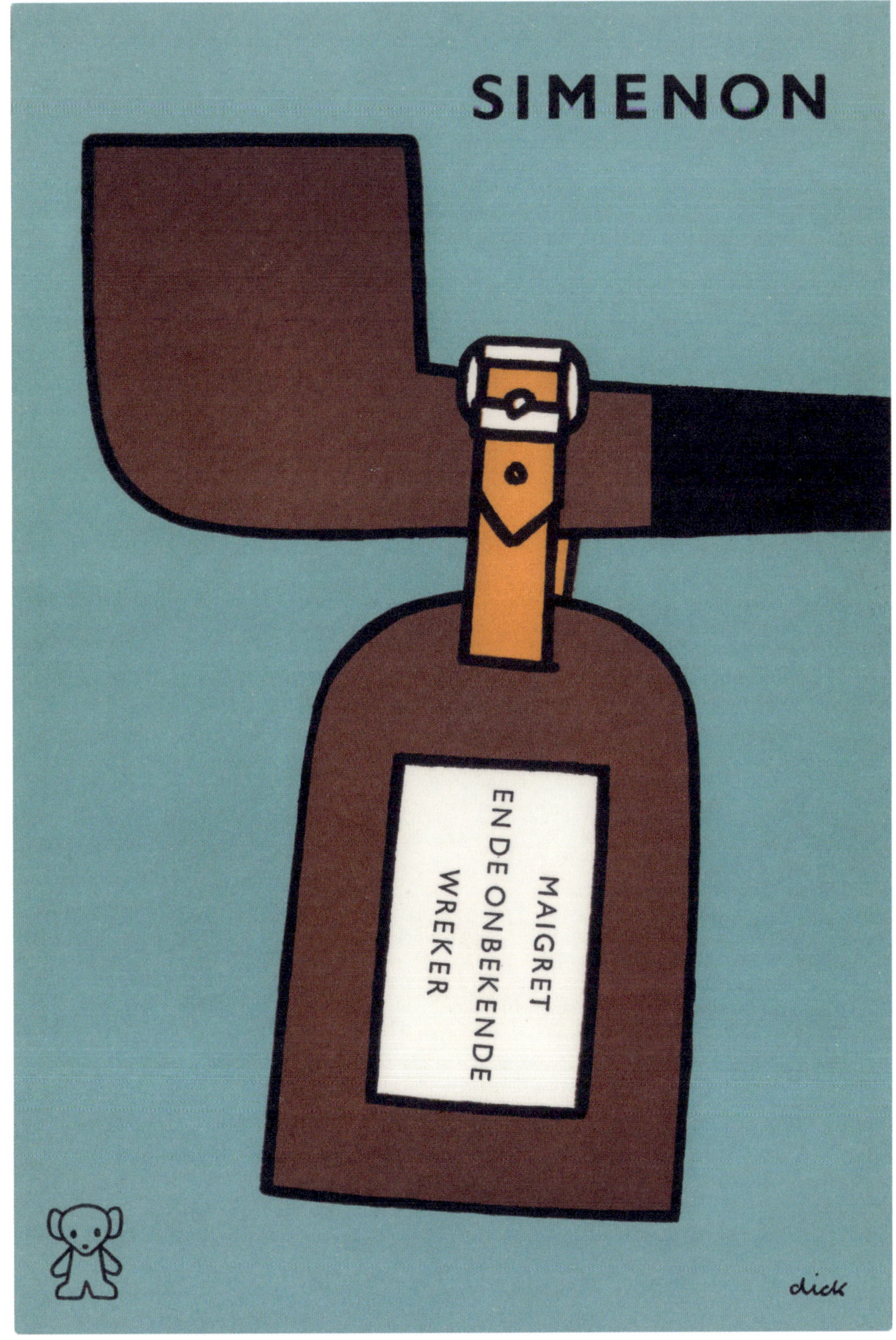

SIMENON
MAIGRET
ENDE ONBEKENDE
WREKER
dick

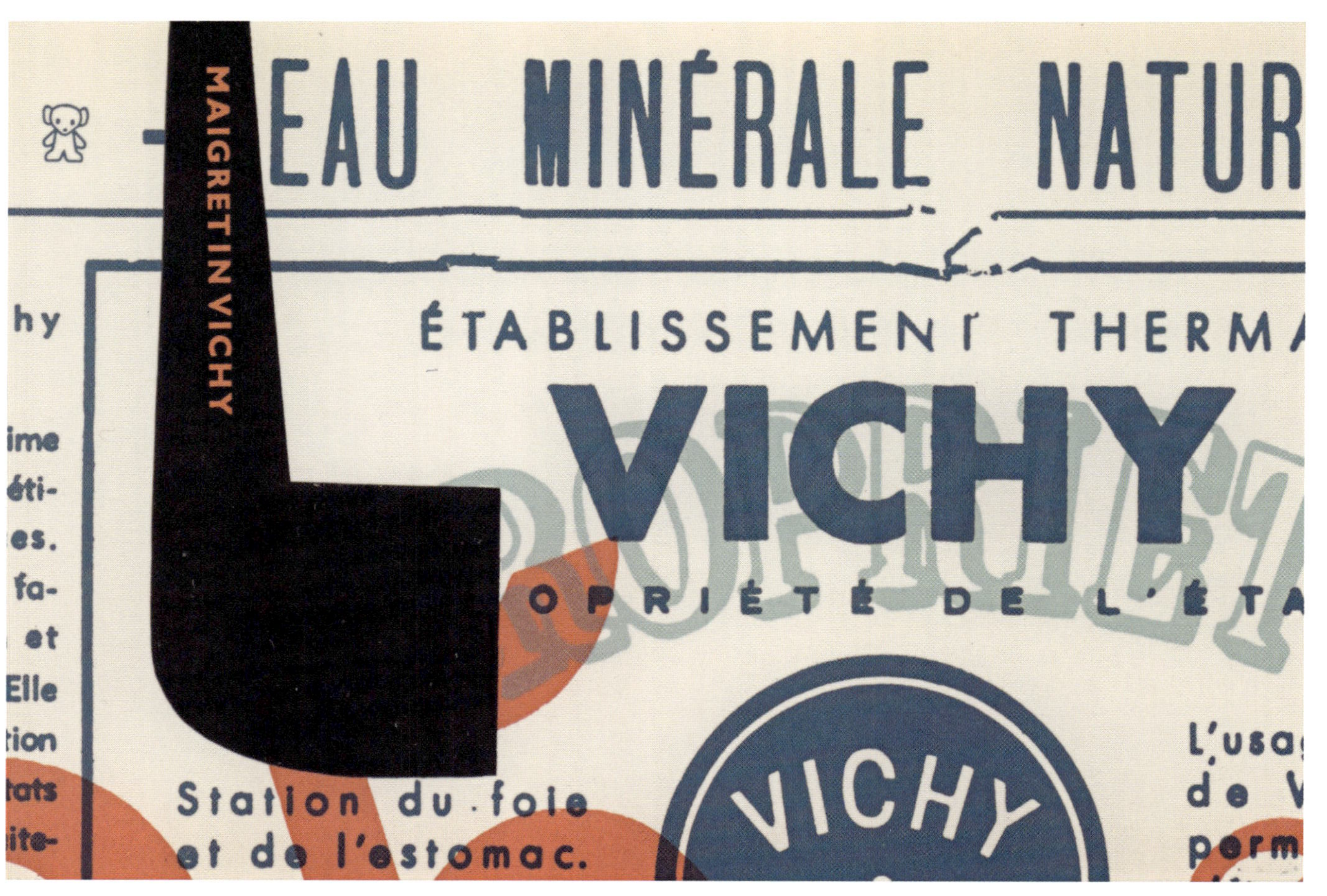
EAU MINÉRALE NATUR
ÉTABLISSEMENT THERMA
VICHY
OPRIÉTÉ DE L'ÉTA
VICHY
L'usag
de V
perm
Station du foie
et de l'estomac.
MAIGRET IN VICHY

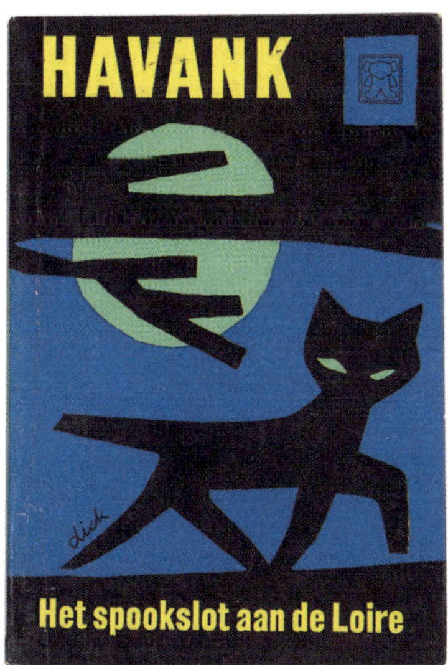

No matter what, Bruna avoided exploiting the grisly elements of these books. It was always about atmosphere not sensationalism. The covers are very much his own with one consistent rule: a book cover must not stand in the way of the reader's imagination.

All the covers were informally signed 'Dick', strikingly simple like the ethos of their design. Was he again distancing himself from the publisher? Was the publisher's name and the bear symbol on the cover enough Bruna for one book?

The Black Bear series proved pure gold for the publishers. These were boom years for A. W. Bruna; the collegial approach of the three men and their ability to commercialize a literary list made the *Zwarte Beertjes* hugely successful. In Bruna, they had a designer with the skills to make their books simultaneously an impulse buy and collectible.

For Bruna's part, he began to apply all the knowledge he had gained on his travels to establish his own artistic style. By 1969 twenty-five million *Zwarte Beertjes* books had been sold across a list of almost 1,500 titles. Bruna would illustrate and design the covers of approximately 2,000 books over the lifetime of the list. In 1968, the company celebrated its centenary and when interviewed about the success of the list, Abs Bruna, in an uncharacteristic show

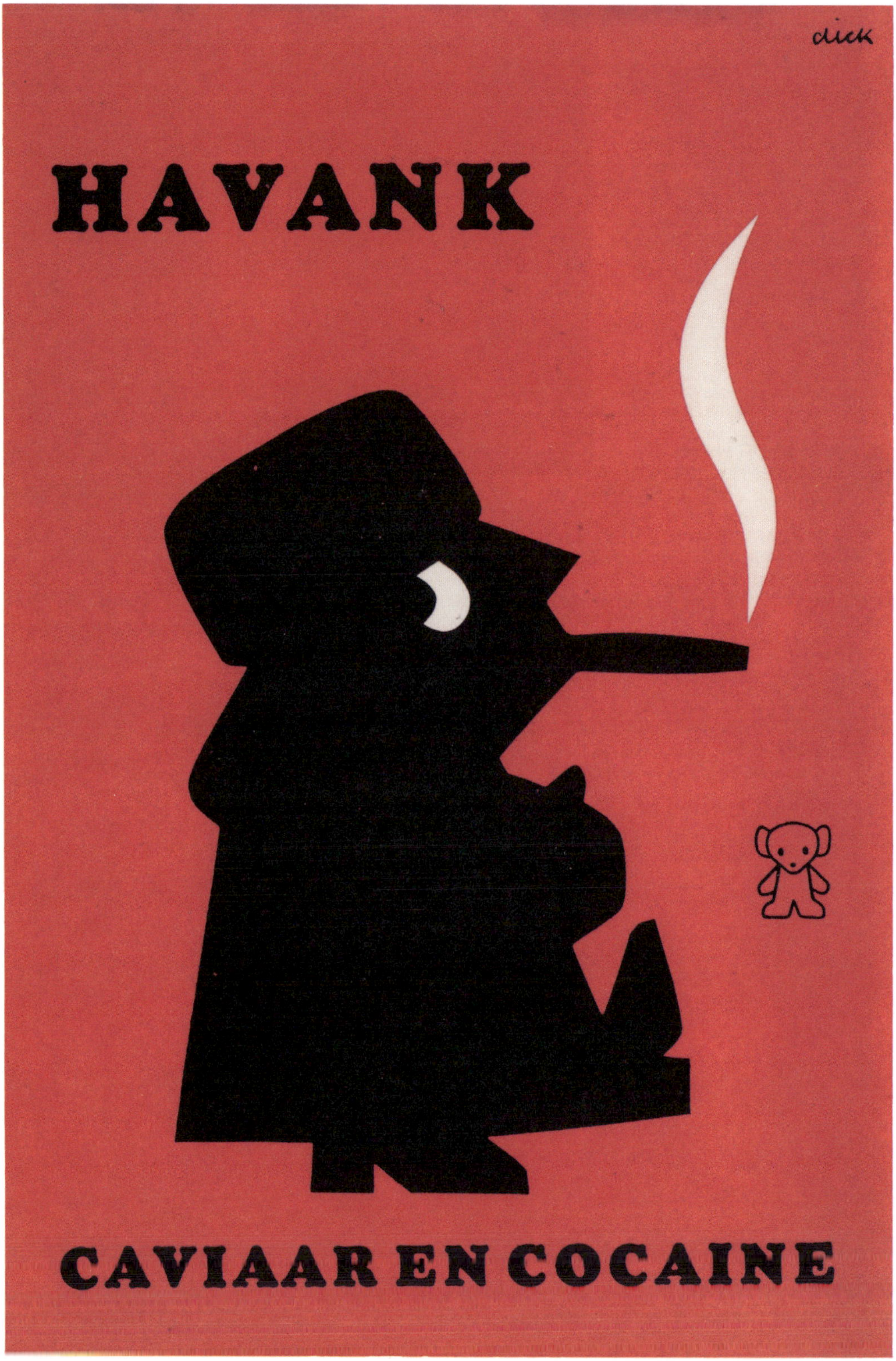

dick
HAVANK
CAVIAAR EN COCAINE

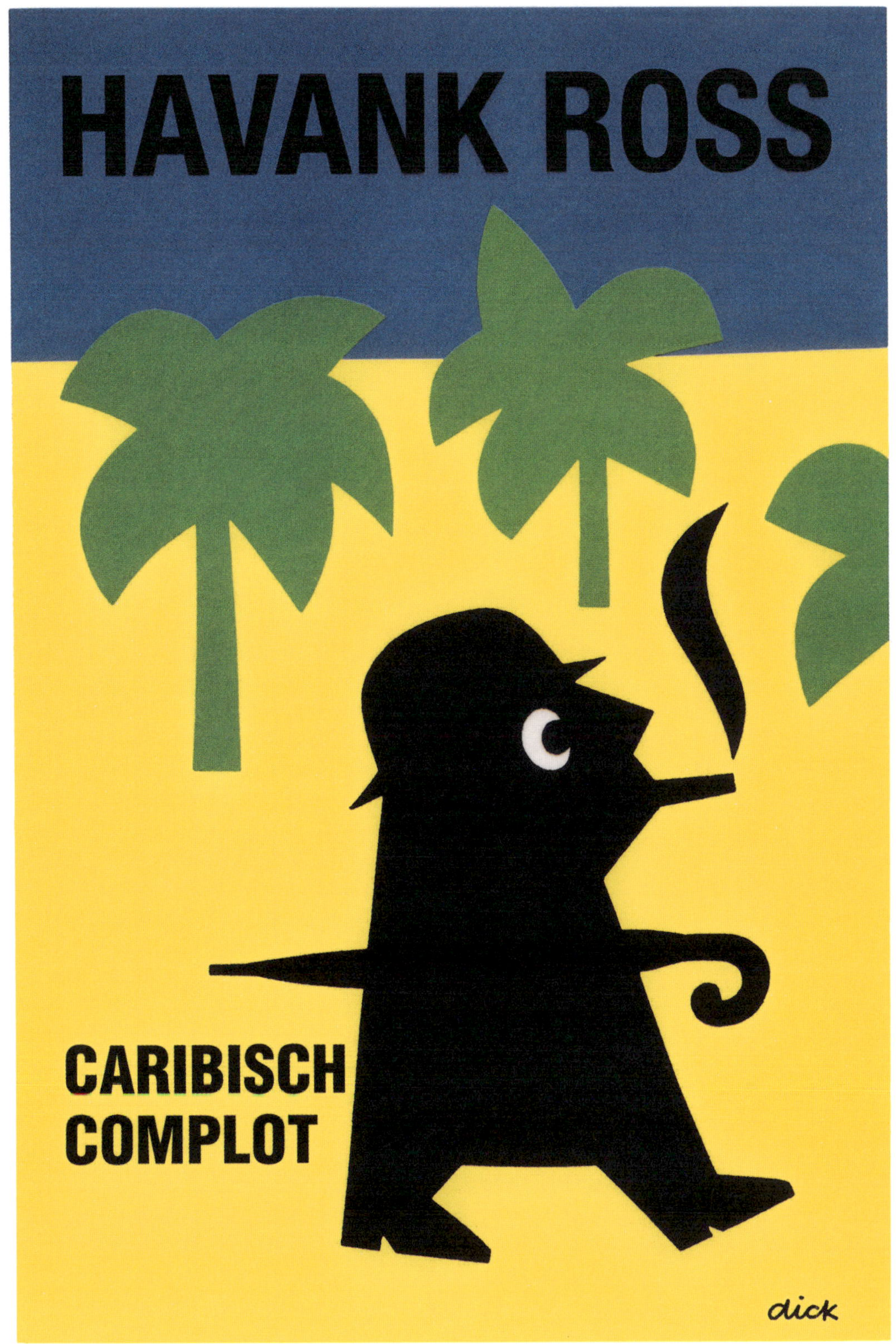
HAVANK ROSS
CARIBISCH
COMPLOT
dick

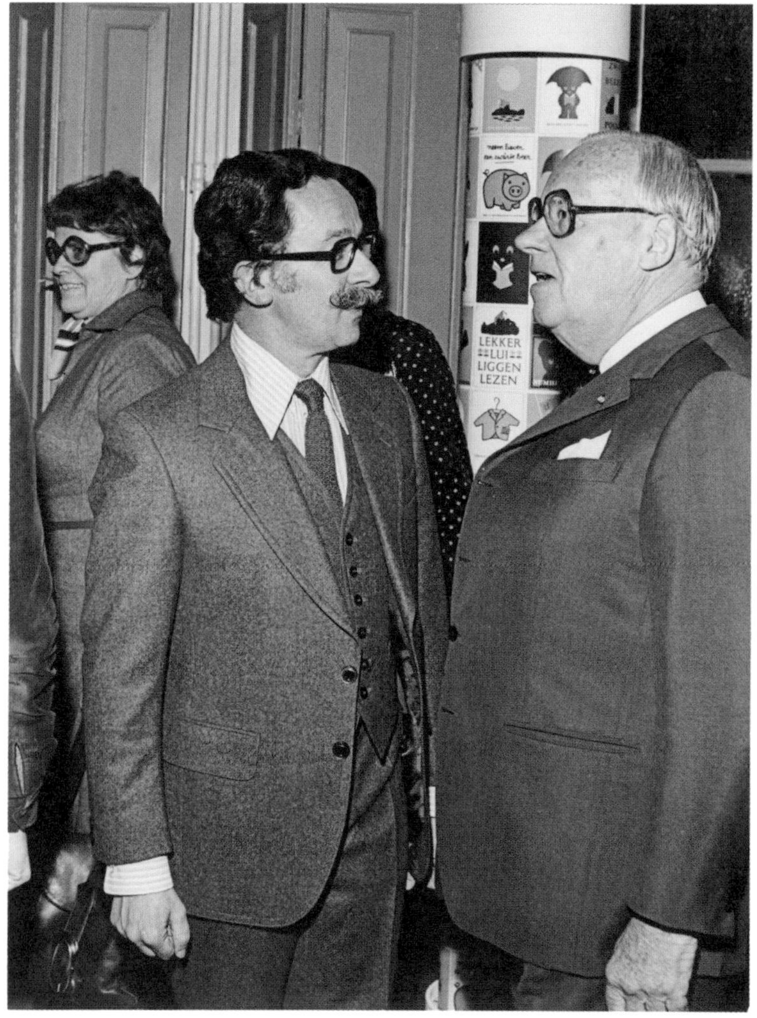

of emotion, declared that, 'all the covers are from the same designer. My clever son.'[25]

The praise did not end there. Bruna had grown up in the publishing world and either knew or was friends with a number of writers, designers and printers, and his covers often received fan mail from the books' authors; Simenon always responded to cover designs as in one of Bruna's most cherished letters: 'The cover you made for my new book is even simpler than the previous one. You try to achieve the same by drawing as I do by writing.'[26]

Bruna with his father, Abs, celebrating twenty-five years of working at A. W. Bruna

Posters

'Simenon once told Bruna that when Picasso saw one of his
book covers he said that it was so effective because it was
approached like a poster. He regarded this as one of the
greatest compliments he had ever been paid.'[27] Bruna loved
posters; his eye for colour and desire for simple impact
meant he had an affinity for poster design and admired
it as an art form.

Willem Sandberg said, 'every poster has to be an artwork',
and Bruna agreed. He saw covers and posters as affiliated
but he spent more time on his poster designs because he
believed they had to score a direct hit. The words of French
designer and teacher A. M. Cassandre were crucial to
Bruna's approach: 'it has to be read at a glance. It must
have the effect of a blow.' Bruna added his own sentiment
to this: 'it must also be human, and, if at all possible,
friendly.'[28] He saw it more as a soft punch.

So here we have it, Matisse's gong; Cassandre's blow;
Bruna's humanity.

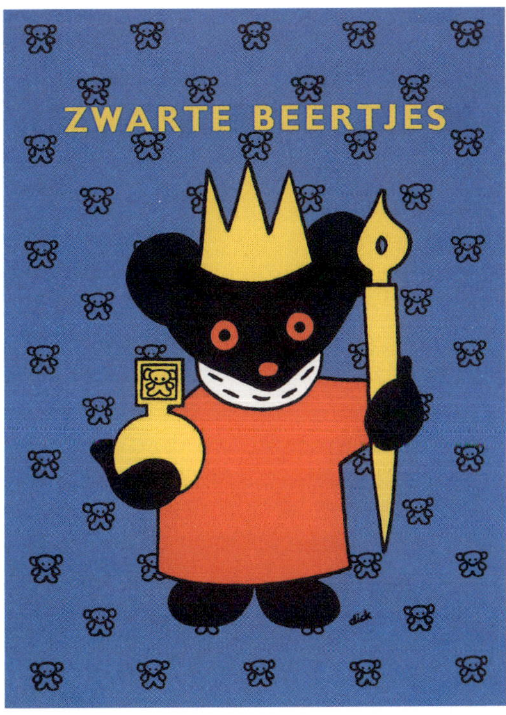

The first poster for *Zwarte Beertjes*,
1956

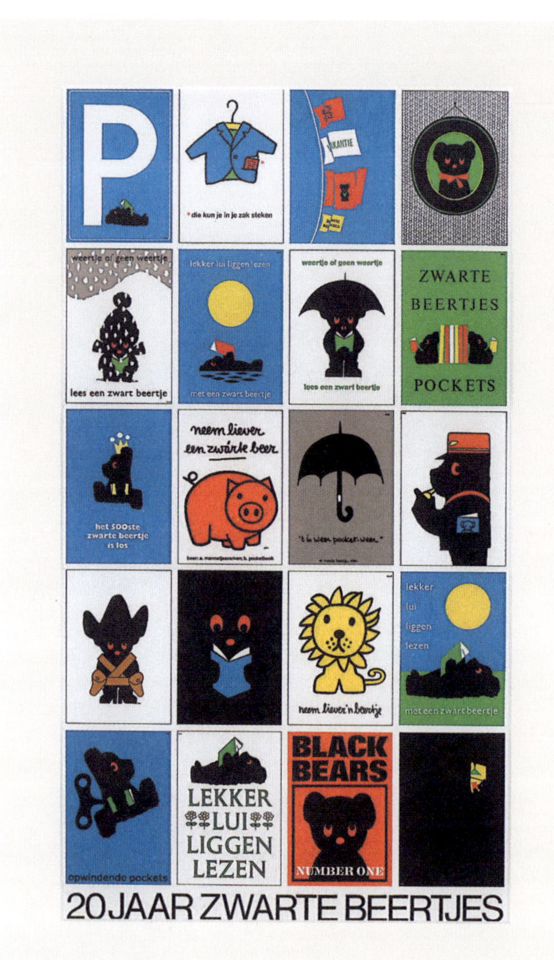

The Charlie Chaplin-inspired humour and simplicity of Raymond Savignac's posters also impacted on Bruna. Apprenticed with Cassandre, Savignac was self-taught and Bruna would have seen his work on display in Paris. He defined poster art as 'the creation of a fleeting image which people will not forget'.[29] Bruna designed and illustrated a poster as early as 1947 but it is the first one he illustrated to promote the *Zwarte Beertjes* in 1956 that epitomizes his objective with poster design. The image is eye-catching and once the bear has lured you in, all the other elements of the message can be taken in quite quickly – impact then detail. Bruna's intention, as ever, was simplicity of form, an ability to convey so much in so little.

ABOVE

Poster marking twenty years of *Zwarte Beertjes*, 1975

OPPOSITE

Poster design for *Zwarte Beertjes pocketbooks voor iedereen* ('pocketbooks for everyone'), 1960

PAGES 64–65

Poster designs for Het Groene Kruis (The Green Cross), 1975

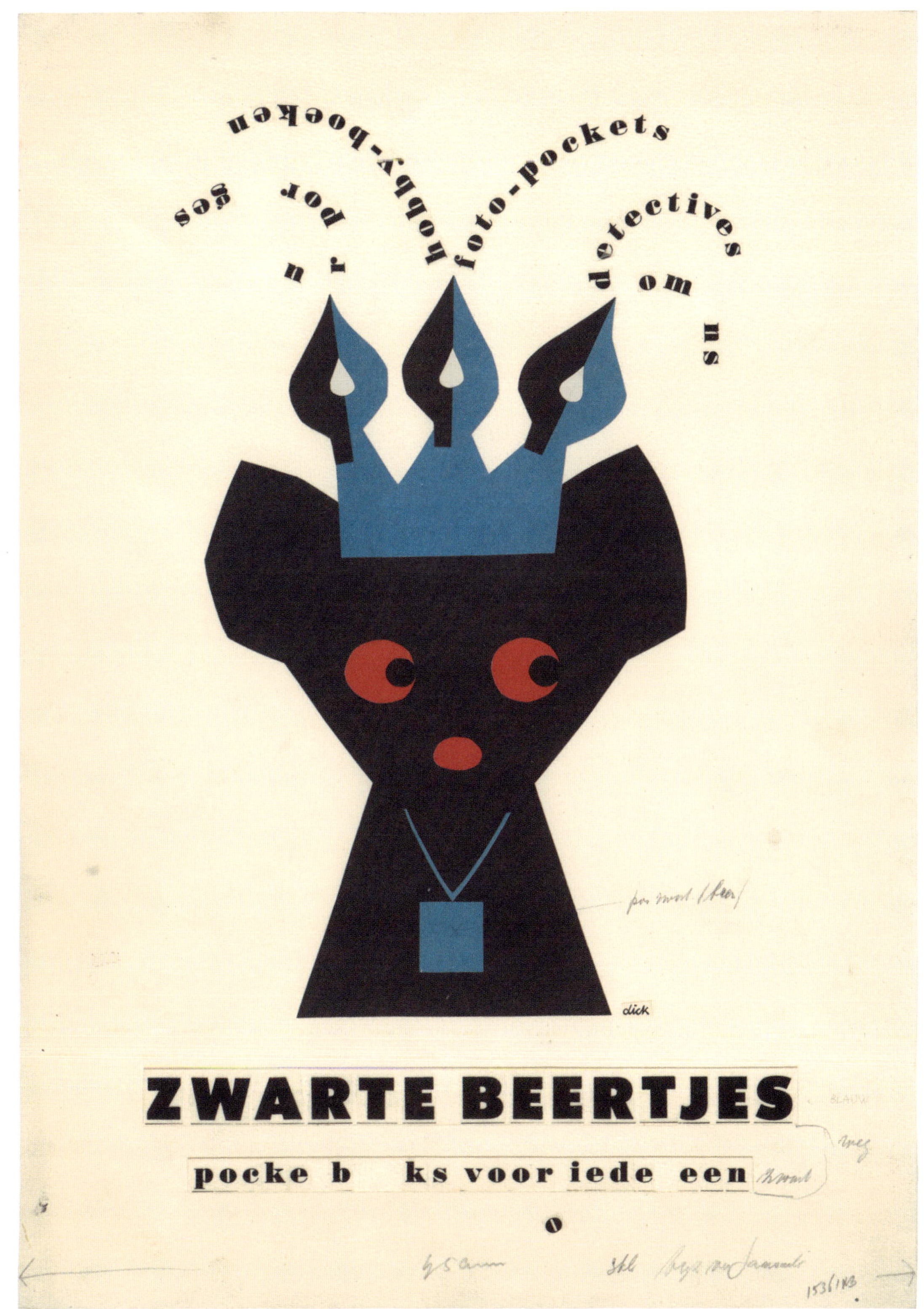
foto-pockets
hobby-boeken
detectives
om u
r por ses
te
ZWARTE BEERTJES
pocke b   ks voor iede een
dick

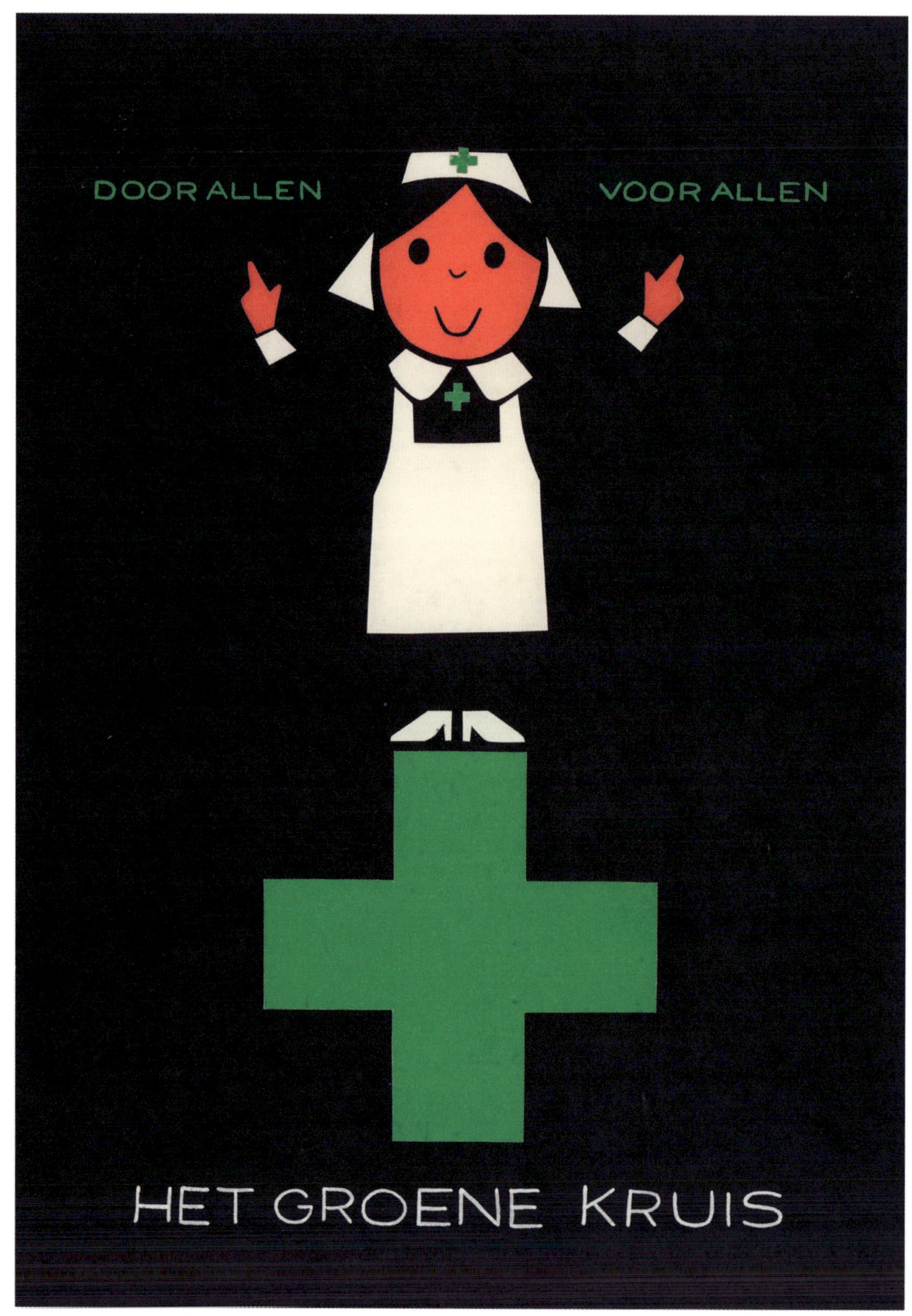

DOOR ALLEN
VOOR ALLEN
HET GROENE KRUIS

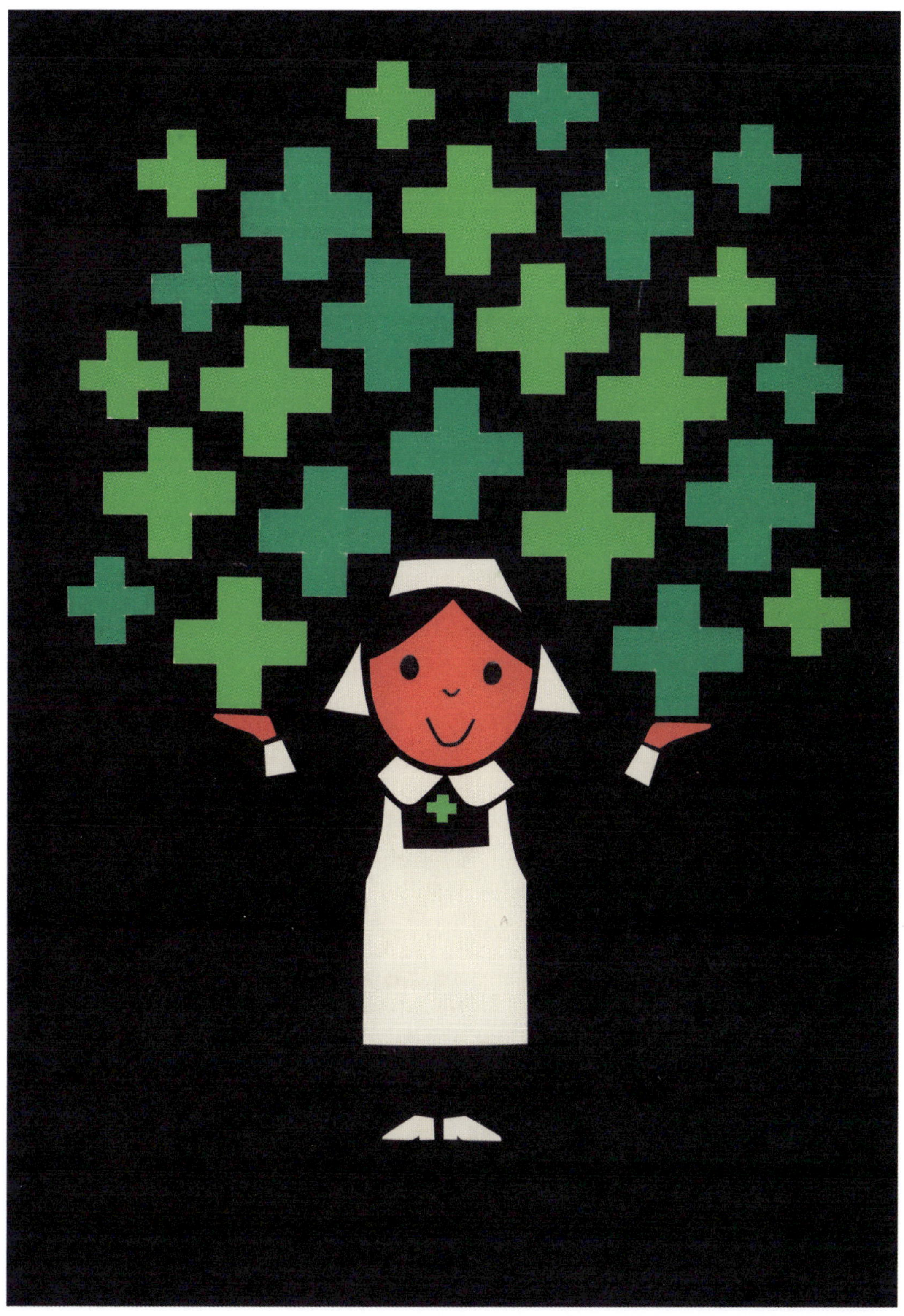

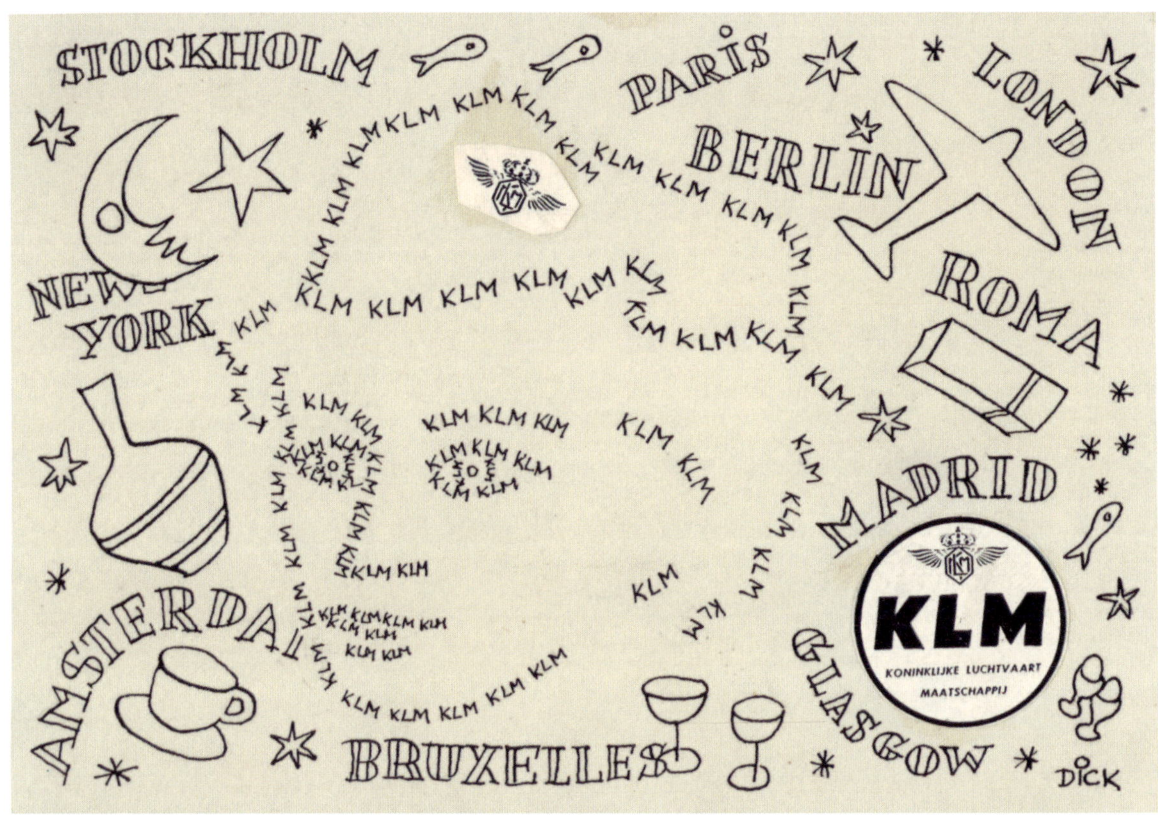

He drew the main elements of the poster with pencil then he filled in the outlines with poster paint and drew the black outlines with a paintbrush. In 1960, a poster of the black bear, red-eyed from reading, won two prizes. Two years later, an exhibition of his work was held at the Clichéfabriek in Utrecht. As the sixties progressed the posters became more graphic and direct, the little black bear almost always staring out to attract attention. Even in a poster with the bear from the side view, he still manages to regard the viewer. Bruna's last poster for the series received a prize from the Advertisers' Association of the Netherlands in 1971.

Design for campaign for KLM (Royal Dutch Airlines); pencil drawing, before 1961

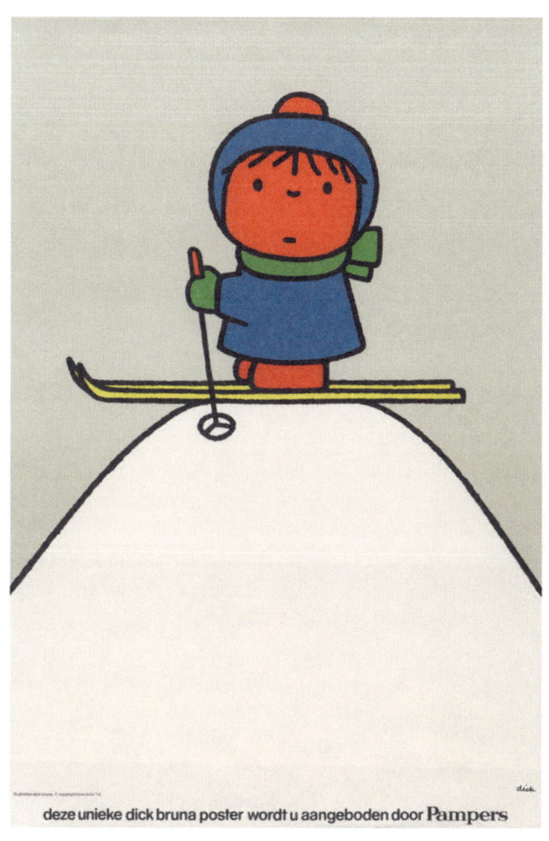

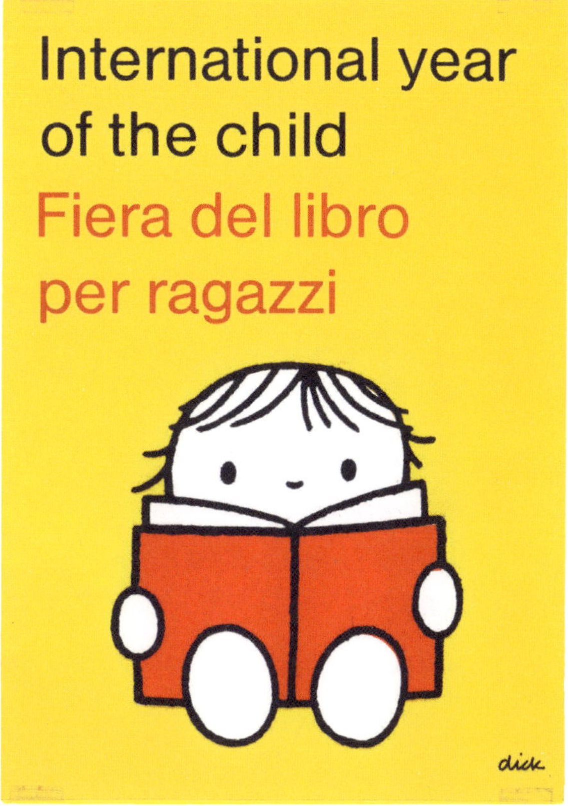

ABOVE LEFT

Poster for Pampers, 1974

ABOVE RIGHT

Poster for the International Year
of the Child, 1979, for the Bologna
Children's Book Fair

Picture books

Newly married and still only in his twenties, Bruna
managed to find the time outside his full-time work to
create books of his own. *The Apple* was published in the
Netherlands in 1953. It was not conceived as a children's
book, more as a homage to Matisse. 'I was full of Matisse at
the time.'[30] The Chapel in Vence was still very clear in his
mind. 'When I saw those cut-outs I thought: This is it. You
should try to make an album this way. And that became
The Apple.'[31] The shapes were cut out and added to by brush
with black paint; only the use of the colour blue as receding

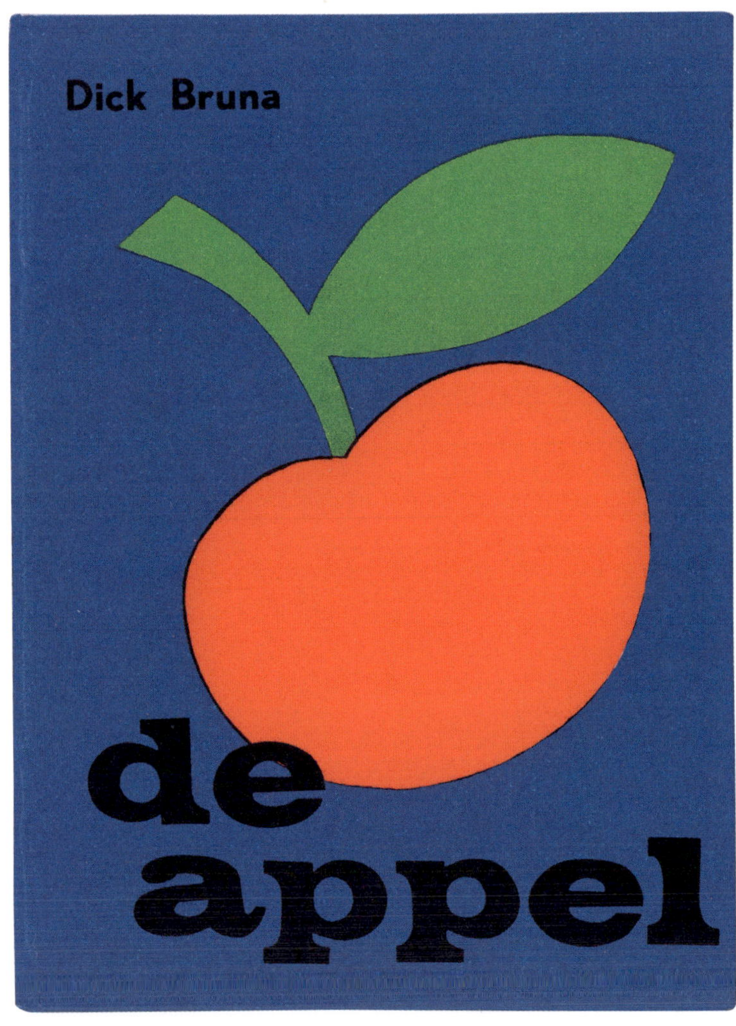

Bruna's first children's book,
de appel (The Apple), 1953

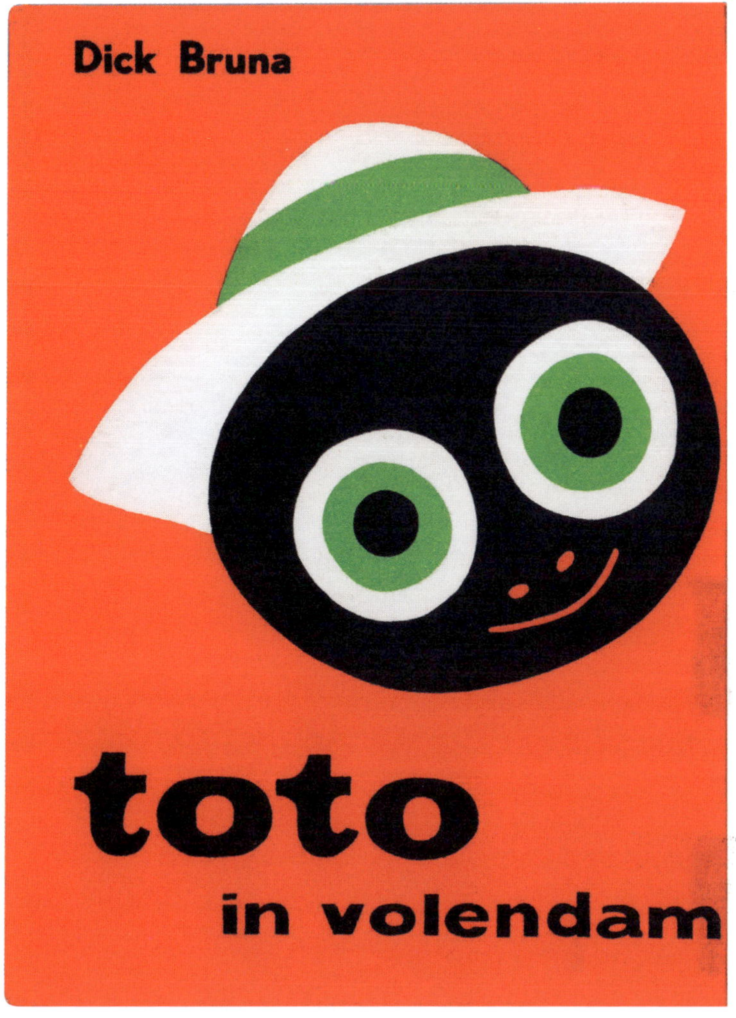

and red as advancing suggest foreground and background. Perhaps the most interesting thing about *The Apple* was what it was not. It was more about technique and less about making a connection with the reader; it was an experiment with form and colour. At the time, the colours were thought to clash, and although Bruna didn't agree with this, it was reminiscent of Matisse's aims in Venice.

The Apple was followed by *Toto in Volendam*, the story of a soft toy that goes for a walk.

The two books are similar in that they focus on journeys of discovery much like those made by their creator at the time. They are important in that they established Bruna's

way of working with a story in his head while he created a
series of artworks. He discovered that he preferred to work
on two, three or even four books at a time so that he could
switch between them, as he did with covers. Throughout the
process he was aware of all creative and practical aspects
of his books.

And then came Miffy…

down to the dunes and sandy beach
and then to see the sea[32]

In 1955, Bruna, Irene and baby Sierk took a holiday in
the small seaside town of Egmond aan Zee, somewhere that
reminded Bruna of similar childhood holidays in the Belgian
coastal town of Blankenberge. Sitting on a rug on the sandy
grass the family watched as a little rabbit skipped around
in the dunes. Another family might not have paid much
attention to this but Sierk had a little woolly rabbit and
Bruna was reminded of his own love of rabbits and a warren
he had made in the garden in Zeist many summers before.

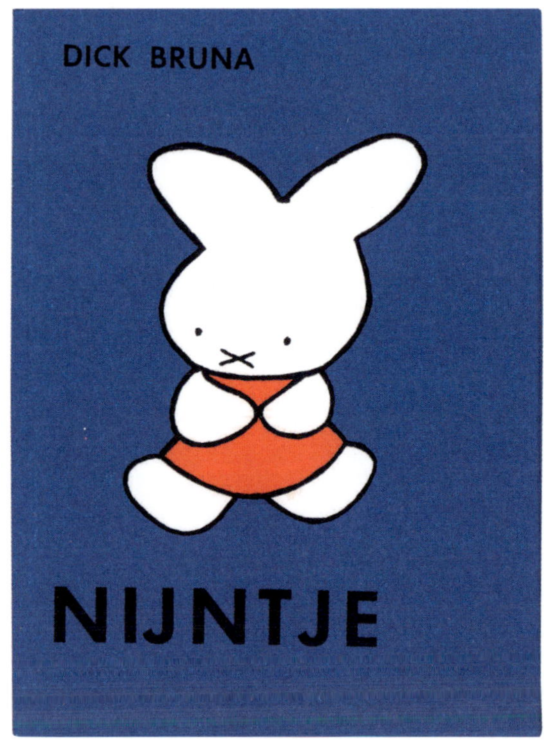

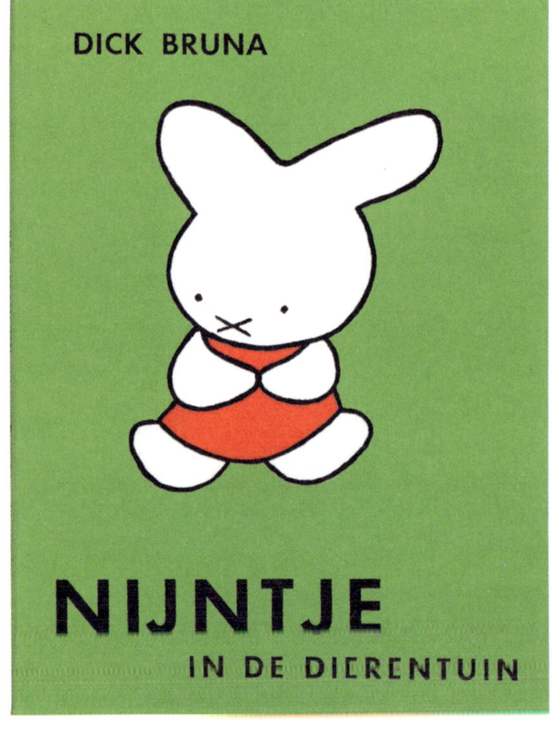

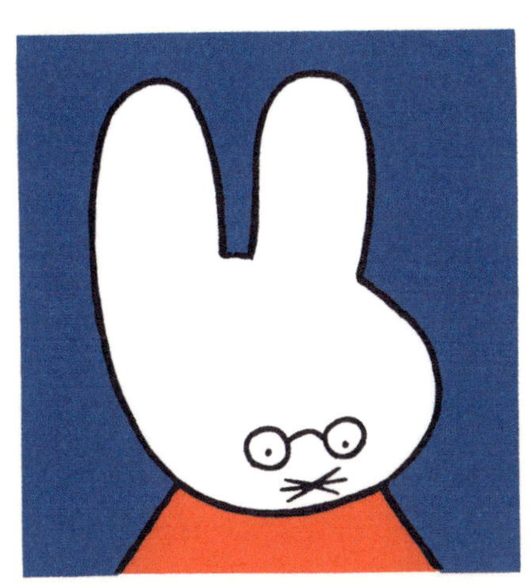

zij mocht met moeder en met vader

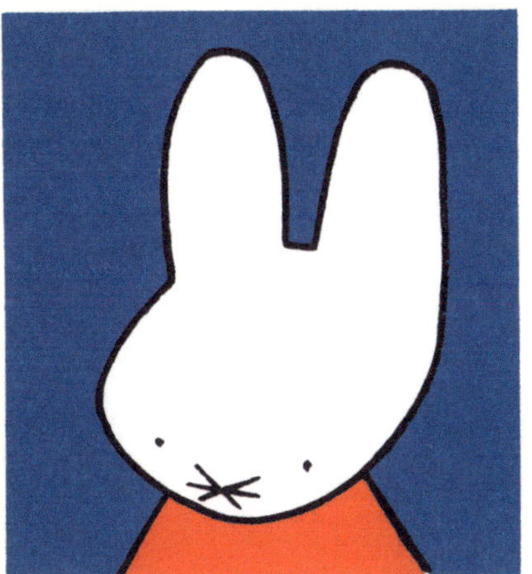

naar de dierentuin toe gaan

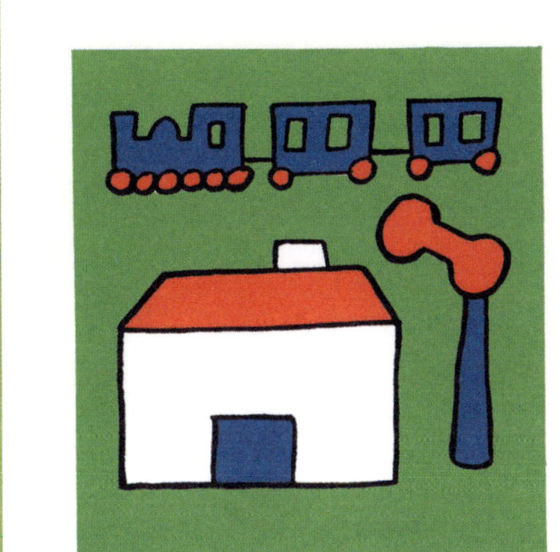

eerst gingen zij naar het station toe
kijk, daarachter stond de trein

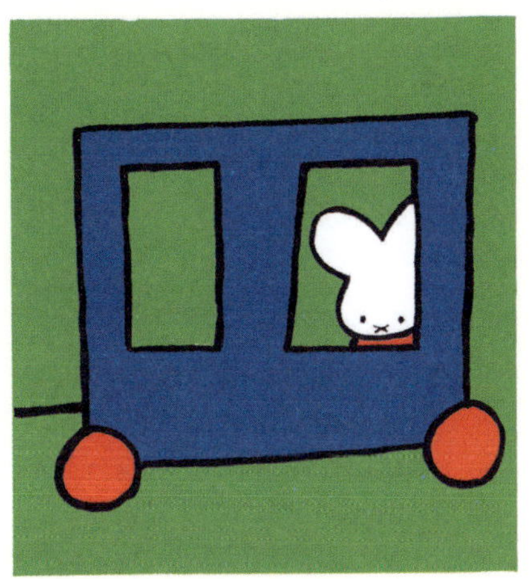

zij stapten in de laatste wagen
en voor het raampje daar zat Nijn

The original Dutch name for Miffy, *Nijntje*, is a shortening
of *konijntje* meaning 'little rabbit'. That first night when
Sierk was told a bedtime story featuring the *konijntje*,
21 June 1955, marks Miffy's official birthday.

The early drawings of the rabbit were a distant relative
of the Miffy the world would come to love. To begin with,
this rabbit looked more like a flat cuddly toy, with a little bit
of Léger and Matisse mixed in. Bruna explained that 'you
want to make something that conveys the idea of a rabbit…
the drawing is like a memory'.[33] Notably, the ears were
askew and the eyes looked away, not yet communicating
with the reader. Mr and Mrs Bunny's expressions made
them look shy and modest, possibly reflecting the humility
of their creator.

Miffy started out as a girl, though Bruna couldn't explain
why, then she became more ambiguous until Bruna added
flowers to her tunic in 1970 for the book *Miffy's Birthday*.
However, many of the first generation of pre-1970 fans
continue to believe that Miffy is a boy and later generations
think she is a girl; thus the universal appeal is not
dependent on gender. Crucially, putting flowers on the
'dress' was an artistic design decision, not an intentional
editorial one.

The original books, *Miffy* and *Miffy at the Zoo*, published
in 1955, were created with pencil and brush. Bruna drew
them, coloured them in with paint and finally added black
contour lines. They sit apart from the methods he was
developing for his Black Bear covers but are similar to his

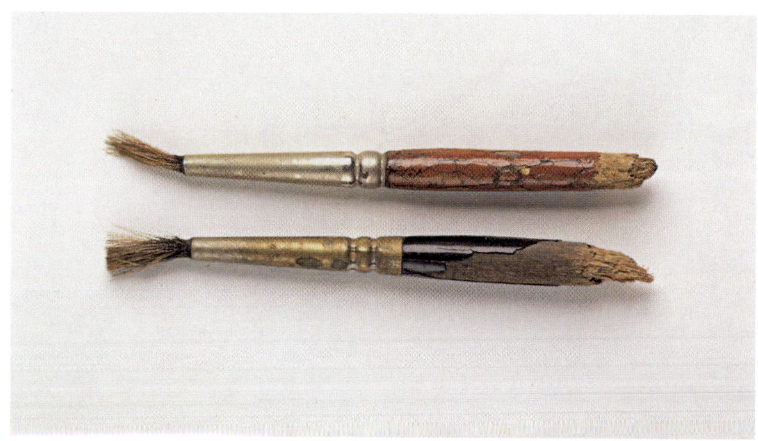

The brushes with which Bruna
painted the first four Miffy books

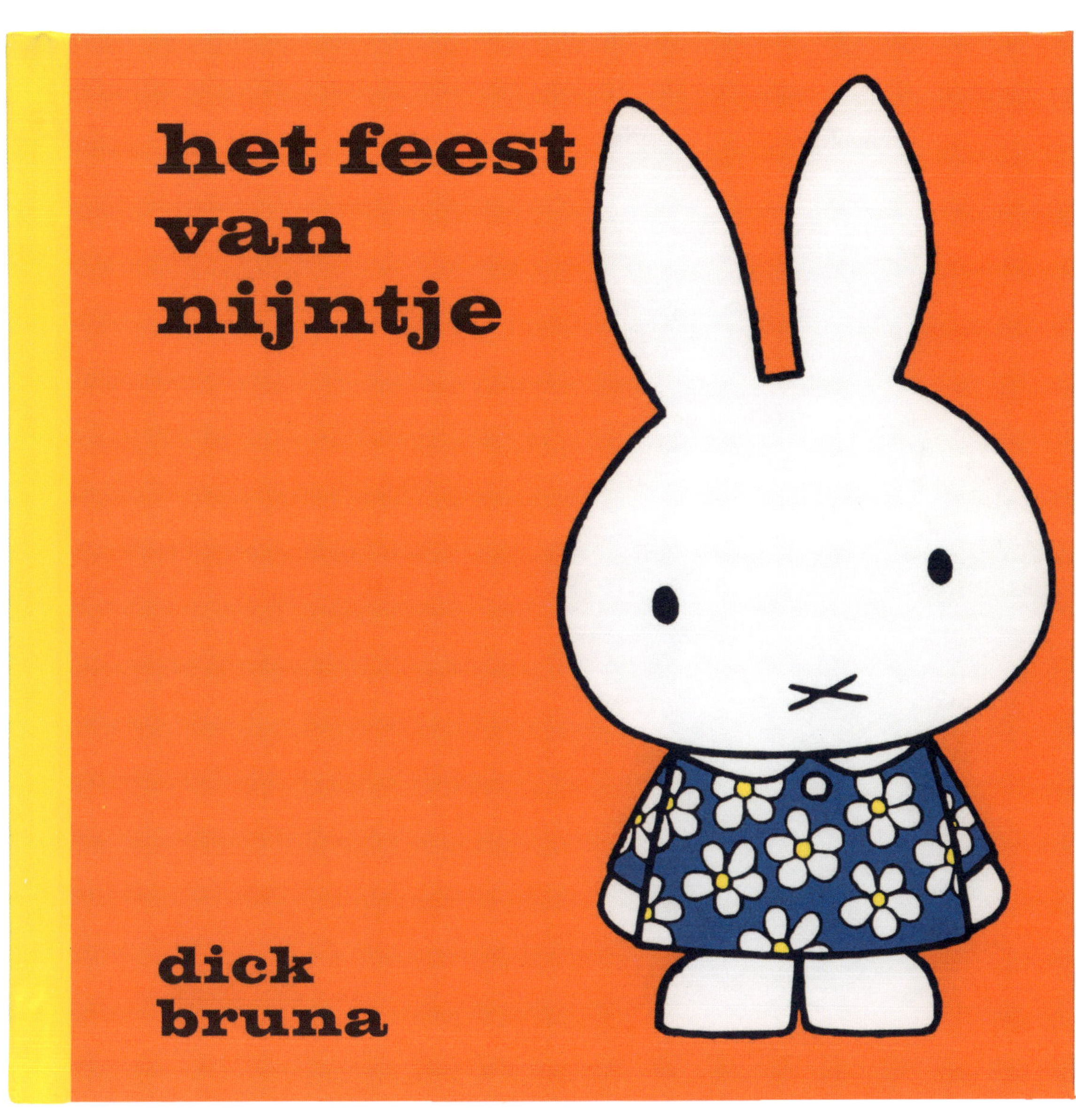

*Het feest van nijntje (Miffy's
Birthday)*, 1970, square format.
Bruna added flowers to Miffy's
dress for the first time

PAGES 74–75

*Het feest van nijntje (Miffy's
Birthday)*, 1970

en o, wat hadden ze een pret

zij balden op het gras

en deden heel veel spelletjes

totdat het avond was

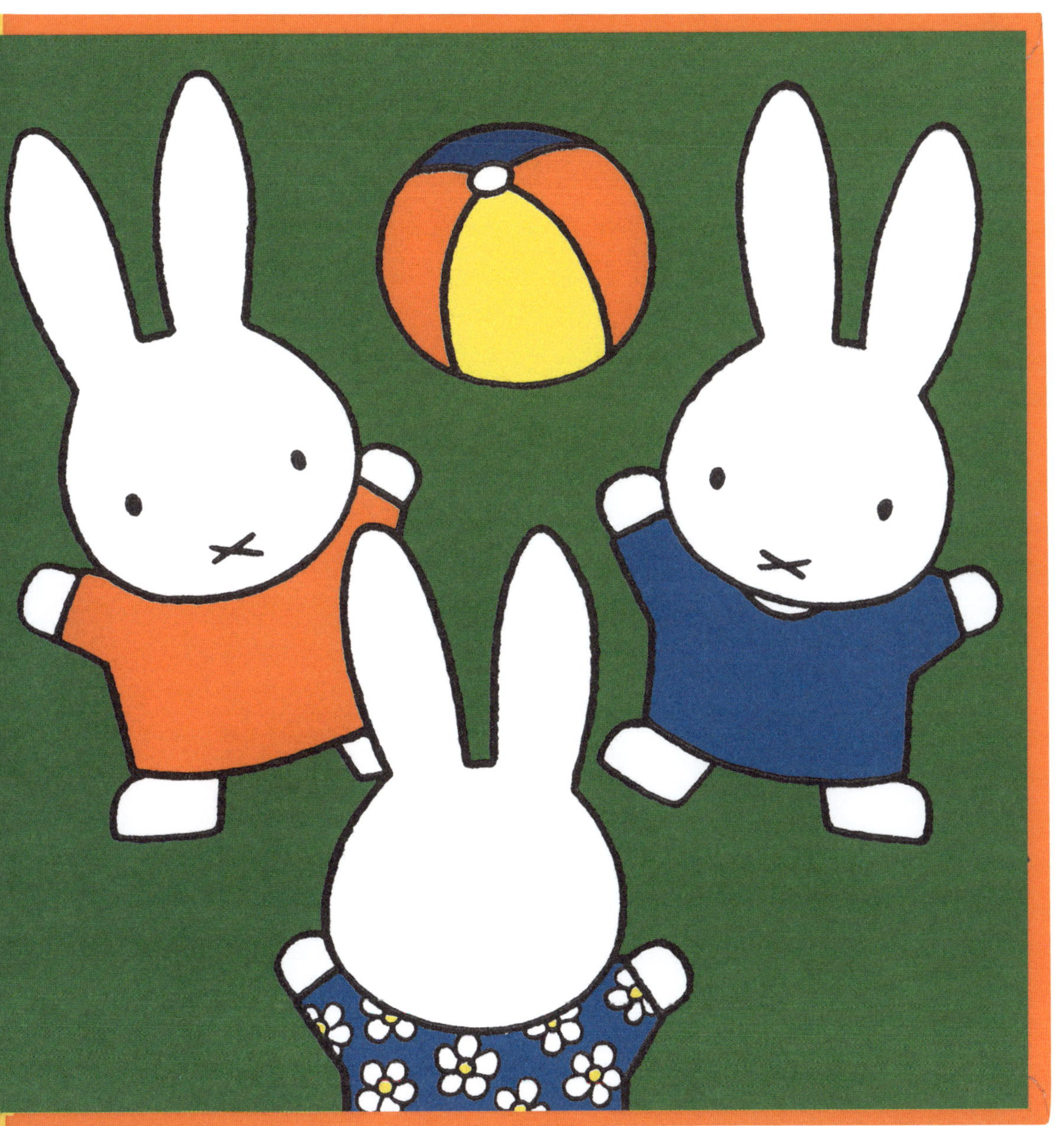

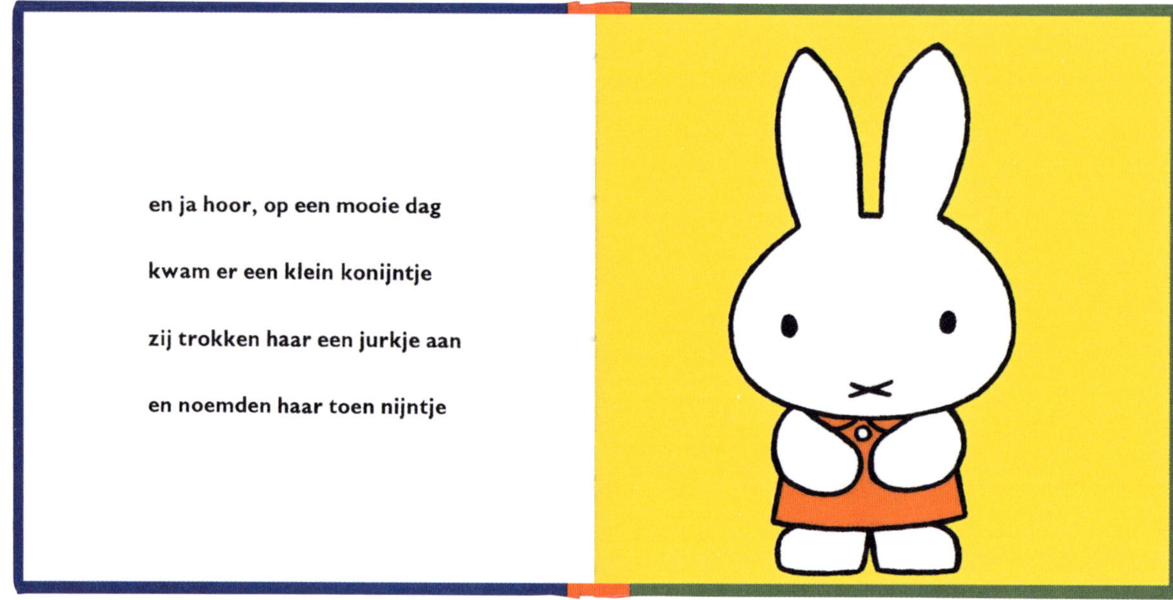

poster technique; they suggest a new father, nostalgic for his childhood. In Bruna's own words, 'Each book belongs to its own time.'[34] 'I was frantically searching for what I wanted and what I could do. I studied and tried out every technique and possibility. I wanted to find my own individual style.'[35] Certainly, these books belong to a time when their maker was venturing in many directions, as husband, father, graphic designer and now picture-book writer and illustrator.

A. W. Bruna was not a children's book publisher; they had no experience of printing or selling them. Children's publishing in the immediate postwar years was largely untapped and undervalued, as were the benefits of reading to children. Since publishers in general were focused on recovery from wartime restrictions, investing in untested genres would have been considered risky. However, Bruna had the backing of Jaap Romijn, his publishing ally and friend. He understood Bruna's ambitions and supported the publication of seven picture books between 1953 and 1957. Most of the elements that would subsequently make the books so successful were misunderstood in the early days; their simplicity, use of primary colours and lack of perspective were in stark contrast to the busier, narrative-led children's books appearing on bookshelves in the fifties.

The first picture books were all rectangular, portrait-format, closer to the dimensions of a paperback than a children's book. They consisted of twenty-three, full-colour, square illustrations with two lines of text under each image in sans-serif lettering, no capitals. Everything was set against a white background. The line is a little more hesitant and the colour more subdued than the later versions.

All change

The first square format book appeared in 1959 as a result
of discussions with Bruna's poster printers, Steendrukkerij
De Jong & Co., about replicating the success of the colour
reproduction of his posters on his children's books. With
Pieter Brattinga, the owner's son, his old school-friend and a
graphic designer at the printers, he worked out that a sheet
of poster paper folded formed a square book, 15.5 × 15.5 cm,
to fit twelve illustrations and twelve pages of text, with the
image on one side and the four lines of story on the facing
page. This perfect format reminded him of the Schröder
House designed by Gerrit Rietveld, his hero of the De Stijl

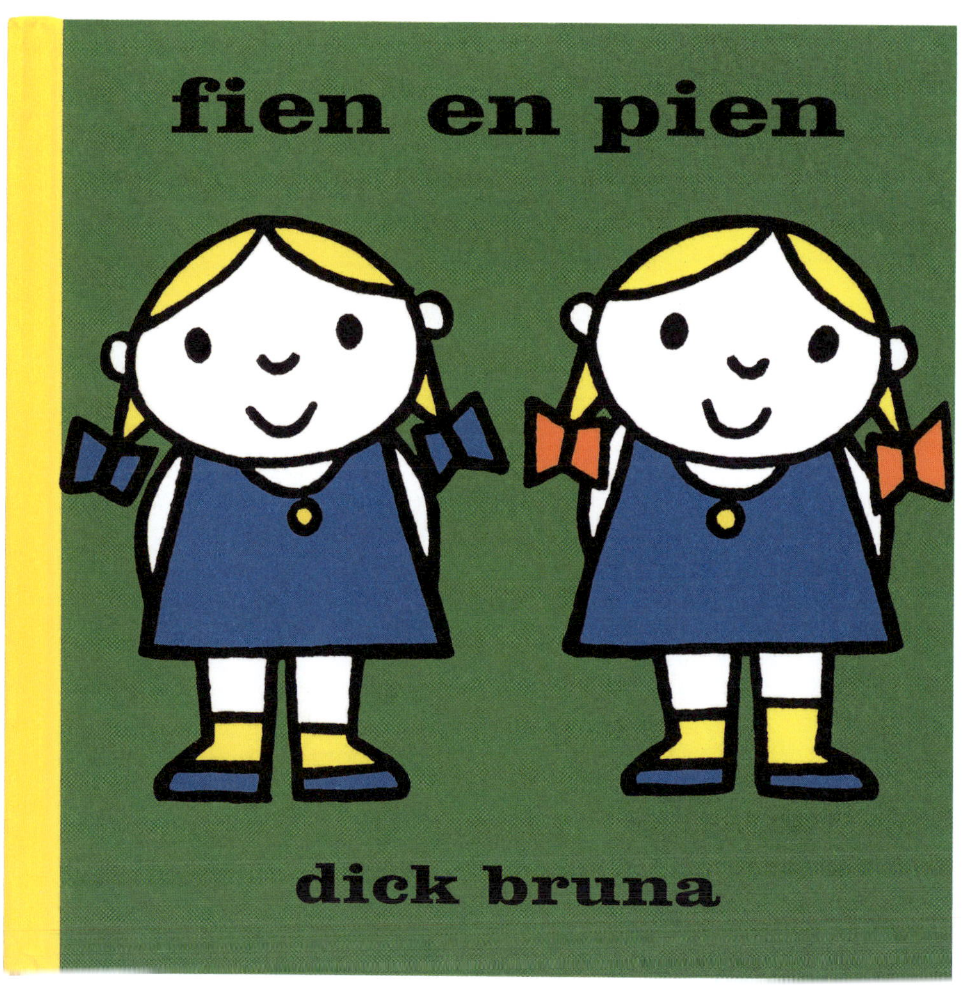

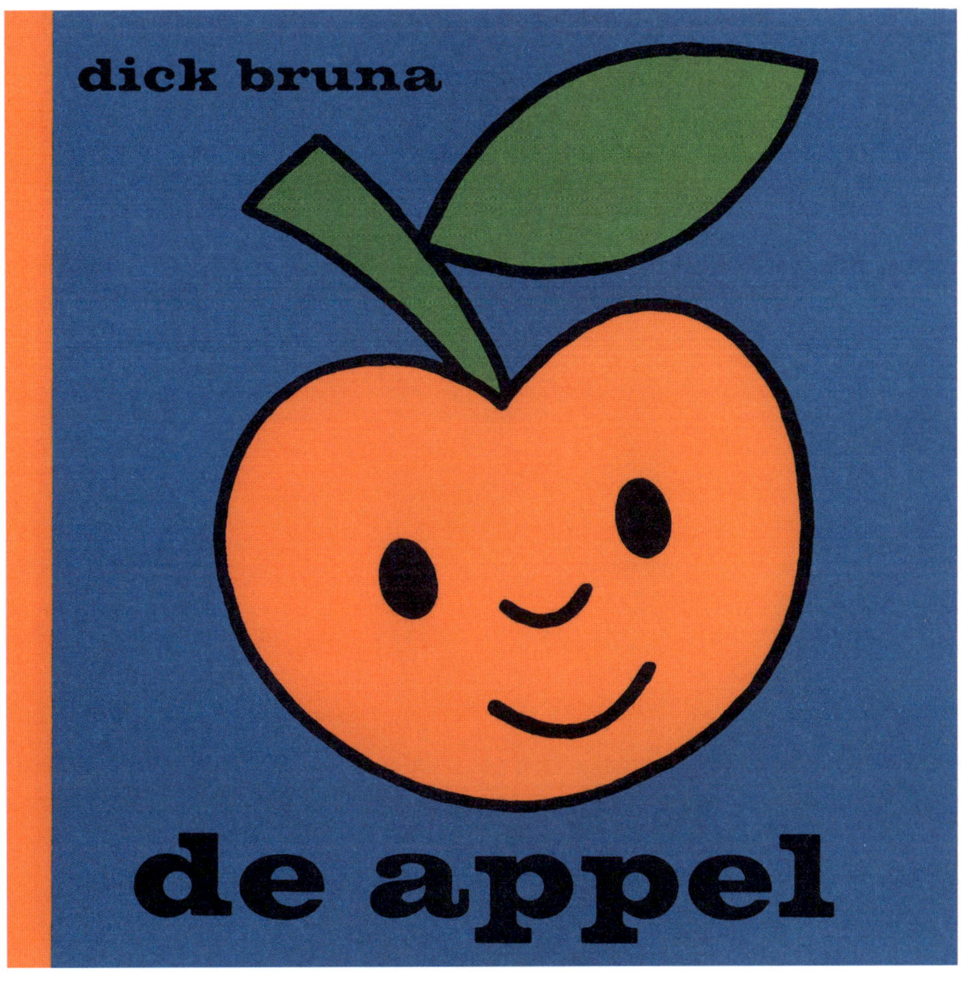

movement. The symmetry and simplicity was excellent; from this time, with few exceptions, the books remained steadfastly square. This format also had the advantage of being economical to print as four books could be printed simultaneously and then sold as a series. This was in keeping with the way Bruna liked to work and a revised version of *The Apple* appeared alongside *The Bird*, *Kitty Nell* and *Tilly and Tessa* in 1959.

The differences between the first and second versions of *The Apple* indicate how much Bruna's work had developed in six years. The square format, brilliant colours, layout of story and illustration, now framed by the size of the book, rather than boxed, all worked for children. His characters

OPPOSITE

Fien en pien (Tilly and Tessa), 1959

ABOVE

De appel (The Apple), republished in the square format, 1959

make direct contact, looking straight out from their
primary-coloured world. *The Apple* has never been out
of print in the Netherlands.

In 1962, the same year the *Zwarte Beertjes* celebrated
their 500th title with an exhibition at the printers, Bruna
produced a second quartet of books: *The Egg*, *The King*,
Circus and *The Fish*.

Miffy returns

Miffy was created for one son, Sierk. By the time the second
versions of *Miffy* and *Miffy at the Zoo* were published in
1963, there were two more children: Marc, born in 1958
and a daughter, Madelon, born in 1961.

It wasn't just the shape and quality of the books that
changed, so too did the way they were formed. Bruna now
fully adopted the method of 'drawing with scissors'. To
begin with, Bruna made a sketch on transparent paper, a
slightly shaky, natural line (Bruna never used a ruler) that
allowed him to try out various shapes and poses. When he
was happy with the drawing he placed a piece of textured
watercolour paper under it and traced over the lines with a
hard pencil so that the outlines were indented into the paper.
Then Bruna used a brush (trimmed to perfect size) to fill the
contours with black acrylic poster paint to bring the figure
to life. The brushwork and paper texture generated his
'line with a heartbeat'[36] animating Miffy and all the other
characters so they didn't appear static. If he made a mistake,
he started again.

When the contours were perfect the drawings were
transferred to film, then came the decisions on colour.
The printer supplied sheets of paper saturated with special
Bruna colours. They may look like primary colours but
are slightly off-primary, containing a touch of black to
distinguish them from standard red, blue and yellow. In a
departure from De Stijl, Bruna added brown and green to
his palette, simply for expediency. 'Grass has to be green.'

Bruna was able to cut out the colours and experiment
with them using the transparent sheet. If one colour didn't
have the right effect, he simply had to try another piece of

Stages of Bruna's working method:
sketches, final traced images, black
contour in poster paint

Bruna at work in his studio at the
Jeruzalemstraat in Utrecht

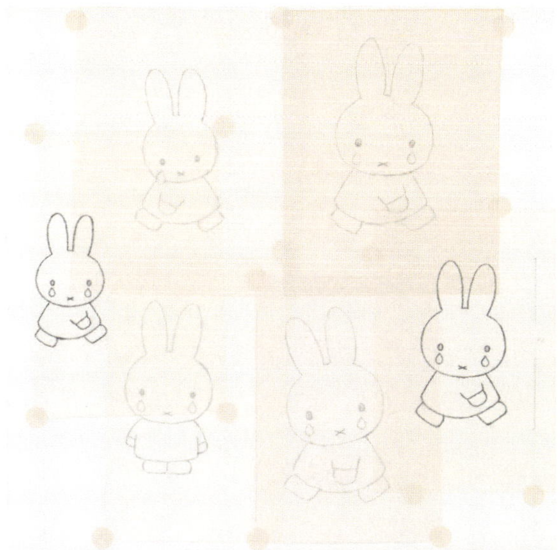

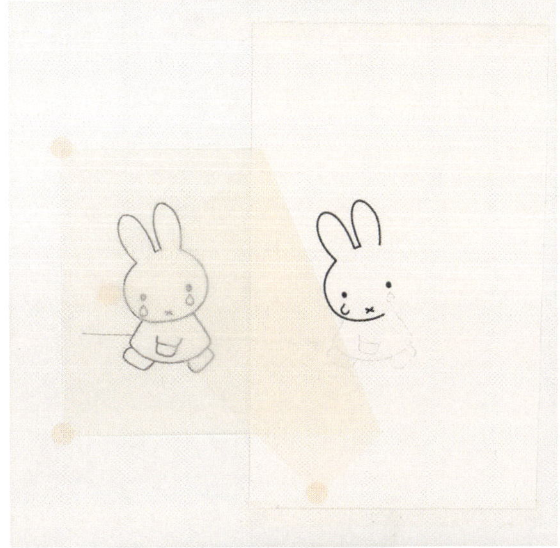

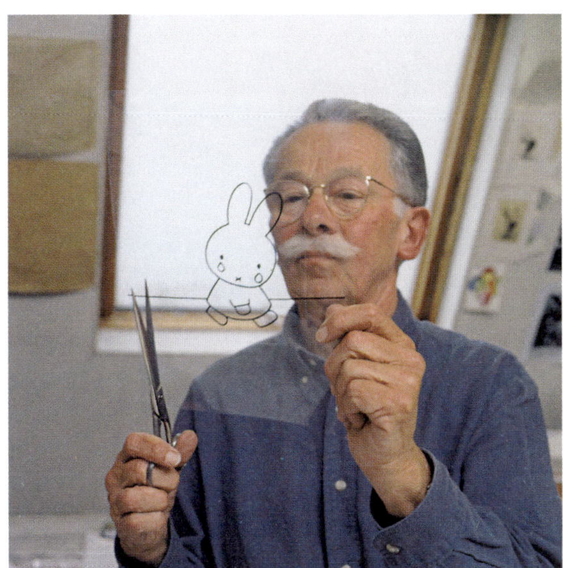

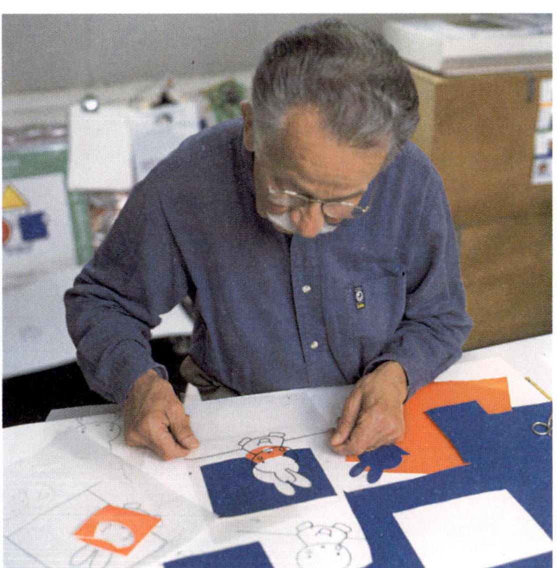

coloured paper. Bruna had seen this technique of moving and replacing pieces of coloured paper in Matisse's book *Jazz*. When all the decisions were made, the sheet with the cut-out colour shapes and the film with the black contours were sent to the printer.

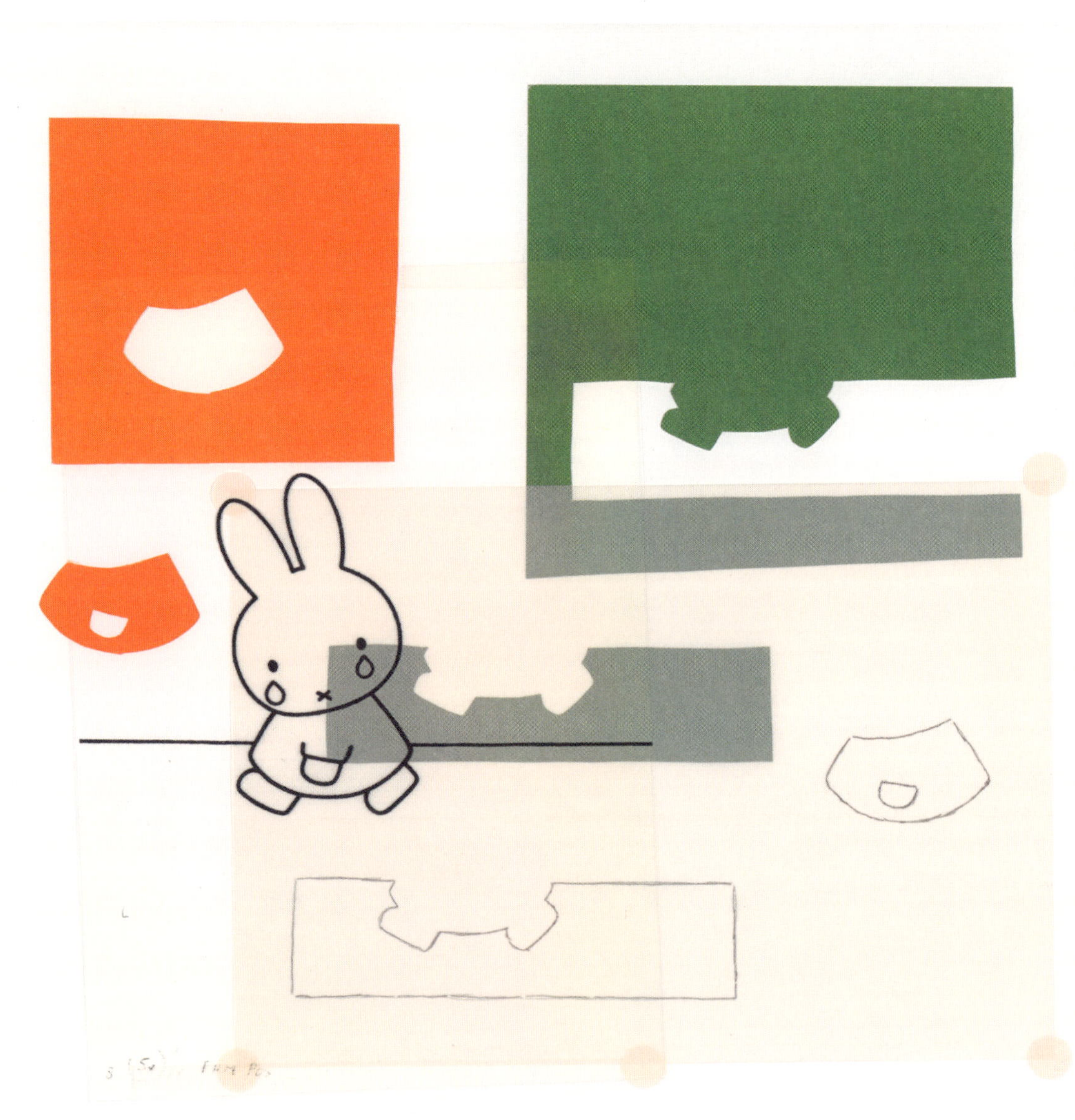

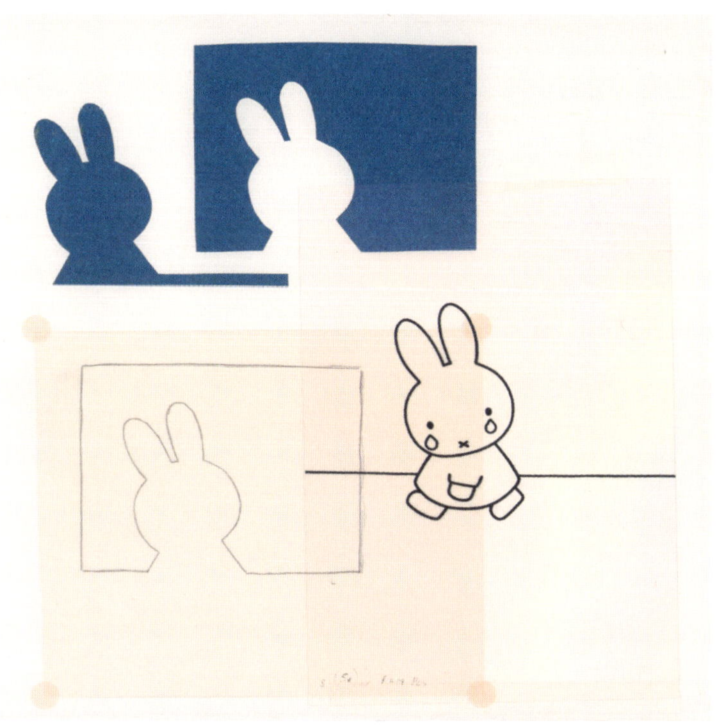

OPPOSITE AND ABOVE

Next stages of Bruna's working
method: black contour drawings
transferred to film, traced images,
his own personal coloured paper
cut into shapes

RIGHT

Final stage of Bruna's working
method: sheet with cut-out
colour shapes and film with black
contours as sent to the printer

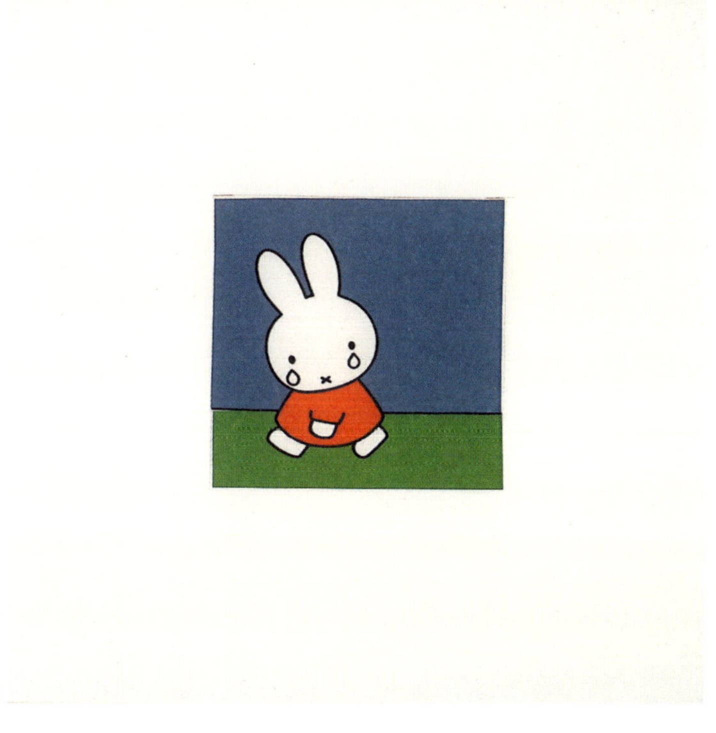

In 1963, Miffy's shape and features changed; the metamorphosis would continue incrementally over the following years but the most dramatic amendments appeared at this time. Her head became more rounded, the general shape flatter, the ears pointed upwards, were sharper and roughly symmetrical. A later version of Miffy became even shorter, rounder, with eyes lower and wider apart. The revised square format of the books prompted Bruna to reconsider the shape of the eyes on all his characters to make them more engaging for the reader. He also gave closer consideration to the shape of the heads in general. As he had learned from his covers, the slightest difference in shape

The evolution of Miffy:
1955–1963–1988–1995–2003

The evolution of Miffy's ears:
1955–1963–1979–1988–1995–
2001–2003

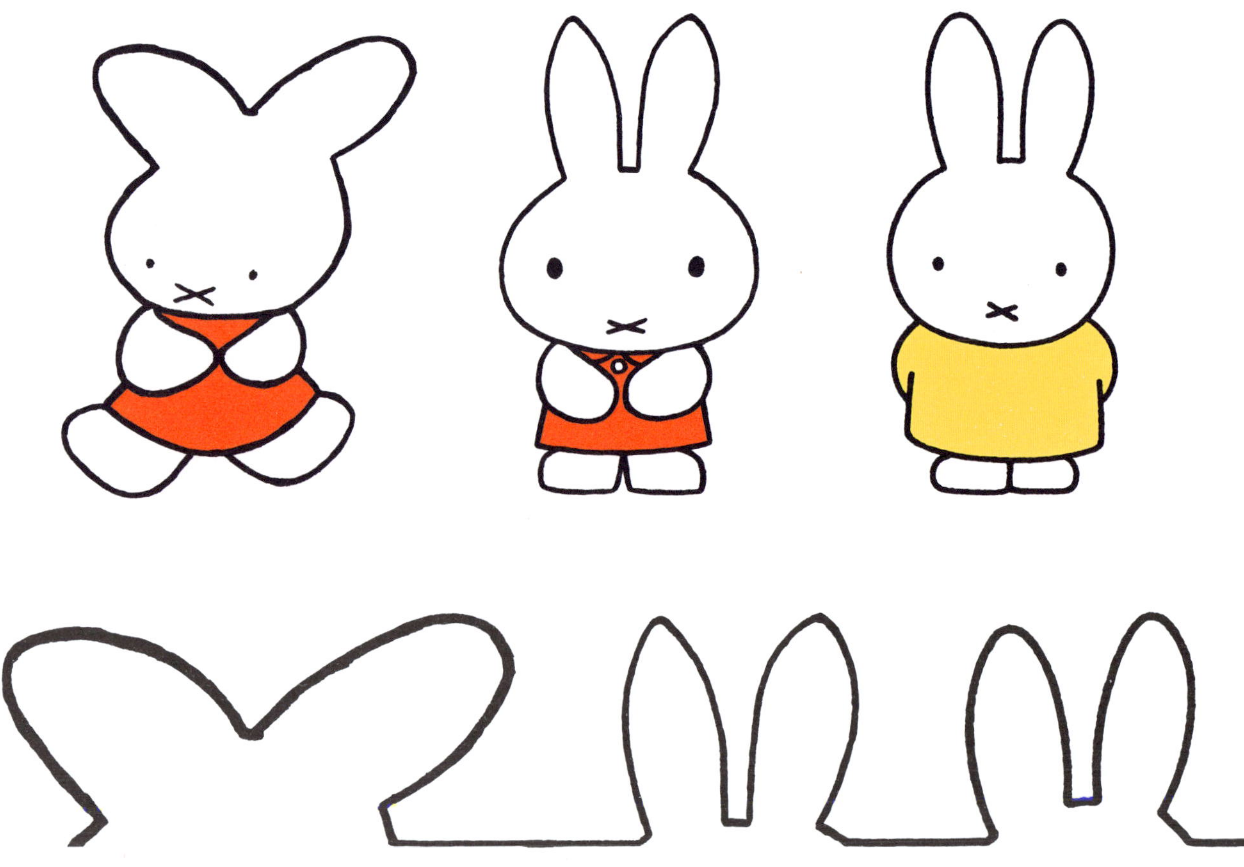

can make a huge difference to interpretation; the thinner the oval shape, the less friendly the character. Bruna was learning more about the possibilities of his visual language and gaining fluency as he went along.

With Miffy's face in particular he was able to convey so much from the slightest change in the two dots and cross for her eyes and mouth. Without this technique to show emotions, Miffy could not have communicated so successfully to her audience. It is a kind of magic. Wim Pijbes, General Director of the Rijksmuseum until 2016, explained: 'Because there is so little, that which is there needs to be perfect. The weight of the line, the positioning of the eye – he creates

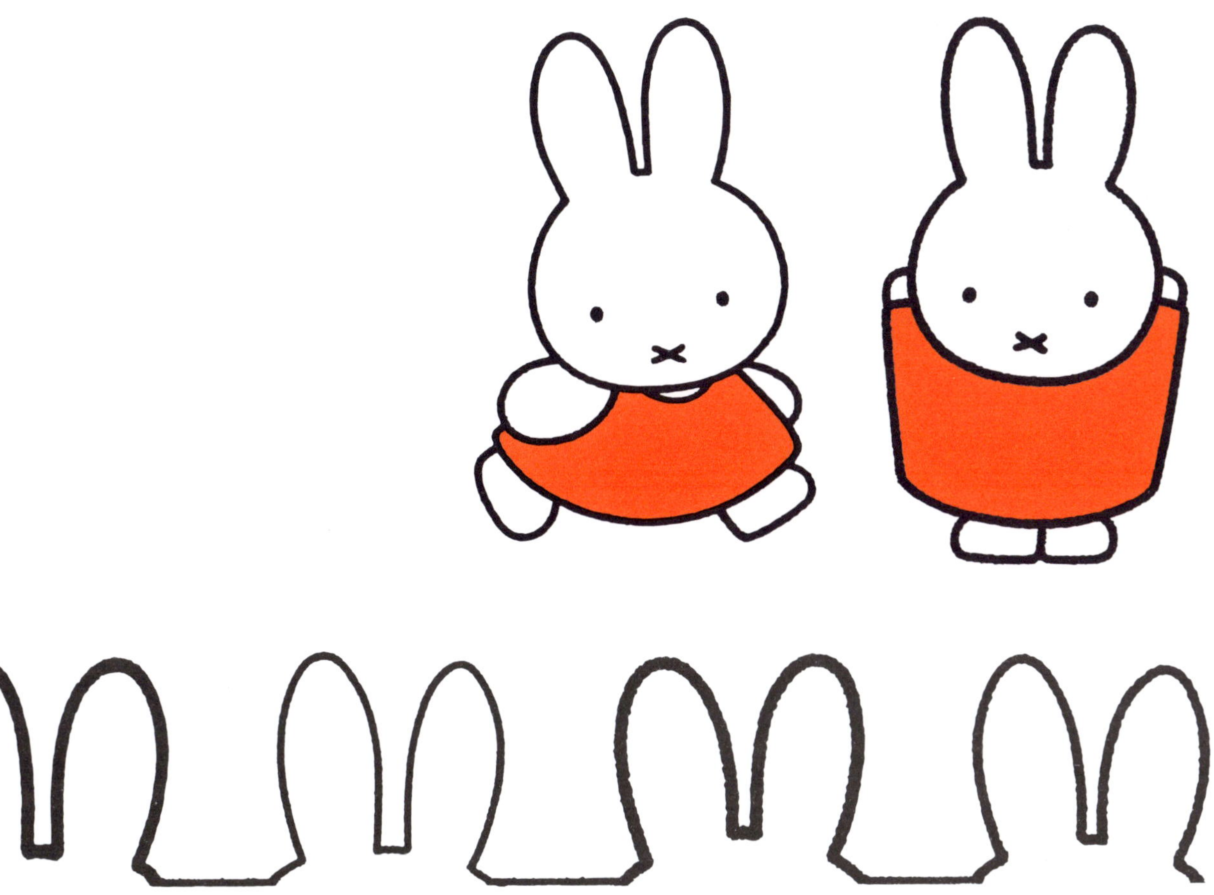

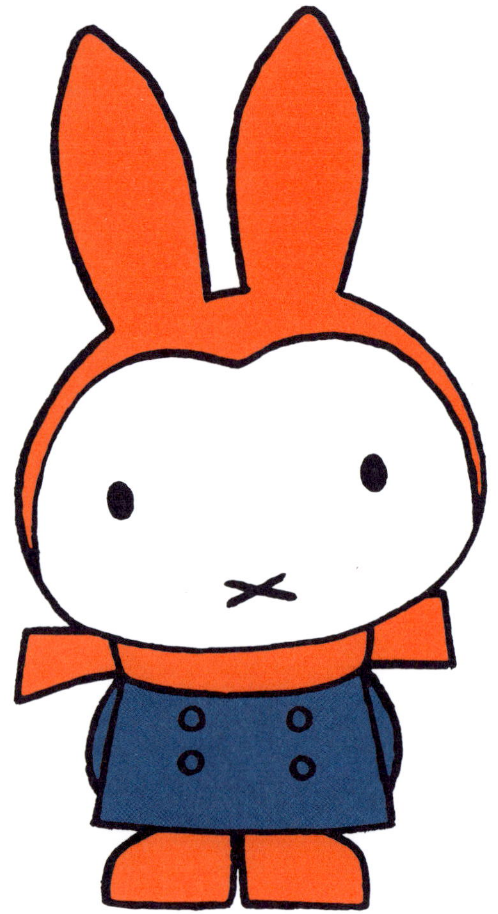

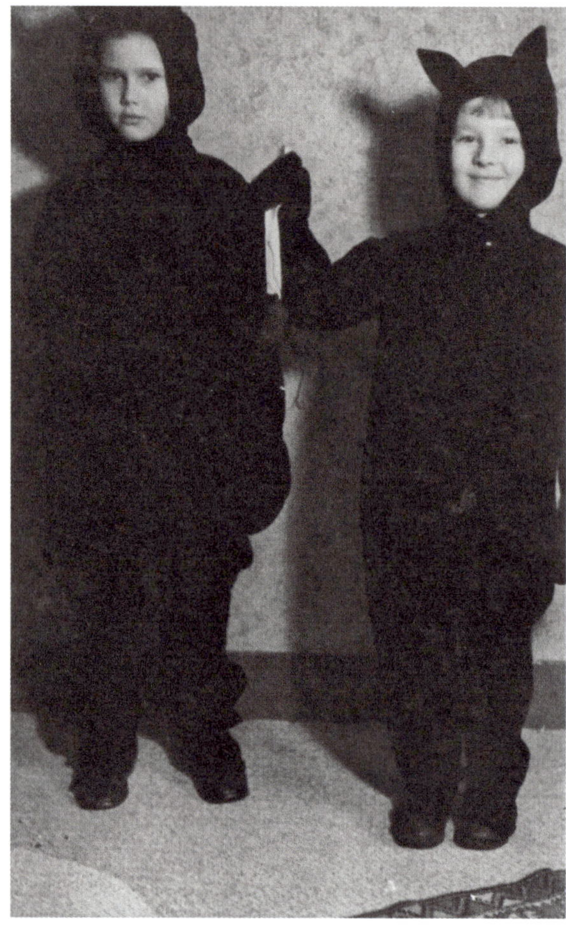

expressions using next to nothing…. The Chinese have an apt expression for this: "Nearly right is completely wrong."'[37]

An experiment to prove this point was carried out at the Rijksmuseum, asking curators to draw Miffy's mouth and eyes from memory in an outline of her face. The results show that even the most visually attuned found it almost impossible.

Some of the changes Bruna made were intentional but often they came from playing; happy accidents that he liked. Bruna did confirm one thing: 'I think my rabbit definitely became more human over the years.'[38] Whatever the grown-ups thought, this was breakthrough Miffy for children, a lovely Modernist antidote to the busy, heavily illustrated alternatives available at the time.

From *Miffy in the Snow*, 1963

Bruna, aged 6, with his cousin Joan

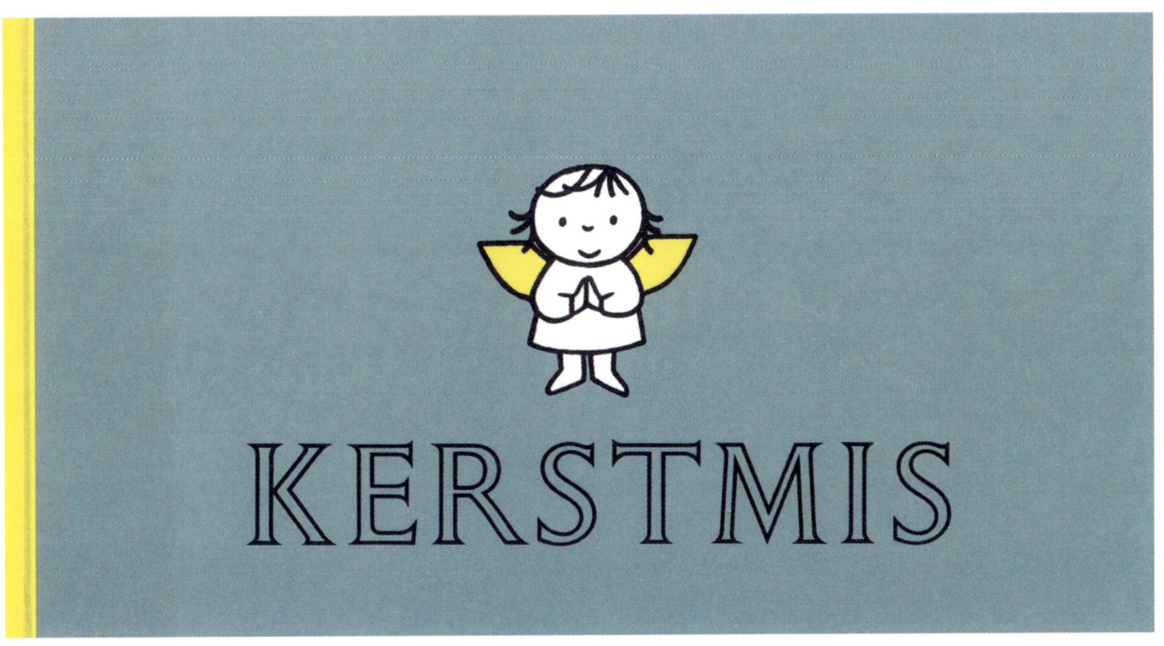

ABOVE

Kerstmis (Christmas), 1963, an exception to all Bruna's rules: rectangular, written in prose, using serif type and not printed in the standard Bruna colours

Miffy in the Snow and *Miffy at the Seaside* were published alongside the new versions of *Miffy* and *Miffy at the Zoo* as well as the *Christmas* book. And in 1963 *Nijntje* was translated into English and became Miffy. Olive Jones, the translator, while in conversation with Bruna, was playing with words that sounded like a rabbit and came up with Miffy. The stories also underwent a change of tack; in keeping with the characters' outward gaze, Bruna started using direct speech in his texts so the reader feels more included in the storyline, a hugely important development.

As with his earlier cover designs, the typeface was the only aspect of the books where Bruna delegated. He always used sans-serif type – as espoused by Willem Sandberg – for its simple minimalist look. There are no capital letters, to ensure the words on the page never conflict with the image; it is lettering without any fuss. Bruna was doing what he felt was right, appealing to the 4-year-old inside him, using the influences he had picked up along the way. Though he didn't know it at the time, he had set Miffy on the path to becoming the world's most famous rabbit.

Writer and illustrator

In 1955, Bruna reluctantly became co-deputy director of A. W. Bruna. But this didn't change his routine; he studiously avoided anything to do with the day-to-day economics, remaining in his creative eyrie on the top floor far from the hub of the office. He was compelled to express himself creatively through his illustrations and he never reconciled himself to the financial workings of 'my father's company'. In 1966, Jaap Romijn, the friend who acted as both buffer from and connection to the commercial side of the business left for the more creative job of Director of the Princessehof Ceramics Museum in Leeuwarden.

By 1970 Bruna had taken on the role of Art Director, gradually giving up designing book covers to oversee the graphic design team. The latest genre was science fiction in which Bruna was even less interested. 'I couldn't read it, I found it very difficult.'[39] He grasped the opportunity to withdraw further from day-to-day involvement and moved out of the studio in the Bruna building. By 1975 the company was suffering a downturn in its fortunes and he stepped away altogether.

The printer Steendrukkerij De Jong had an open-house policy whereby designers would meet up. It was the closest Bruna would come to a designers' social club where they could discuss their posters and designs and watch them on press. Here he chatted with some of the pioneers of postwar Dutch graphic design including Otto Treumann, Jan Bons and Gerard Wernars.[40]

Steendrukkerij De Jong provided another boon to Bruna in the form of Pieter Brattinga, his in-house collaborator and friend. As requests to use Bruna's illustrations on numerous items of merchandise started coming in,

Brattinga understood the implications for the integrity of the characters and the quality of his artwork. As a result, in 1971 the friends founded Mercis bv, the company that would control and guide any spin-off activity. Brattinga became Miffy's official guardian and trustee of the Bruna drawings, colours and copyrights. The pair could have had no idea just what a global licensing business this would become. Fortunately, once again, Bruna was able to stay well away from the business to concentrate on his artistry.

Everything was now in place for Bruna to concentrate on his books and to accept commissions for other work. In 1969, Bruna designed a series of five stamps for the National Post, Telegraph and Telephone Service and in 1972 he made a mural for a new children's hospital ward in Leidschendam. As the seventies progressed, he did illustrations for children's charities and organizations such as Amnesty International. He continued to design and illustrate posters for both local and international concerns including UNICEF. The city of Utrecht was a particular beneficiary of his work as well as local businesses. In recognition of this, in 2007, he was presented with a special Golden Lapel Pin of the City of Utrecht.

Bruna was not only inspired by artists and designers but also by everything and everyone around him, including the man in the mirror. Poppy Pig was inspired by one of his children's much-loved teachers who was not so sure of the honour at first but came to love her picture book incarnation. Snuffy the dog may be considered part Miffy, part Bruna, with those innocent eyes and moustache-like nose. Boris Bear, self-portrait, alter ego, is a shy but amiable creature who is lucky enough to have Barbara to watch out for him. Barbara is smart and practical. 'That's exactly how it is at home,' Bruna admitted.[41] Boris popped into Bruna's head in France, right out of the forest near their summer house. And even when out shopping, Bruna would be thinking of ideas for books. 'There is not anything better than the colours and smells of a French market.'[42] The inspiration for the stories was always close to home or from personal memories, a reflection of his own life experience with three young children. If he wasn't working, Bruna would get fidgety and often Irene would have to send him off to his studio.

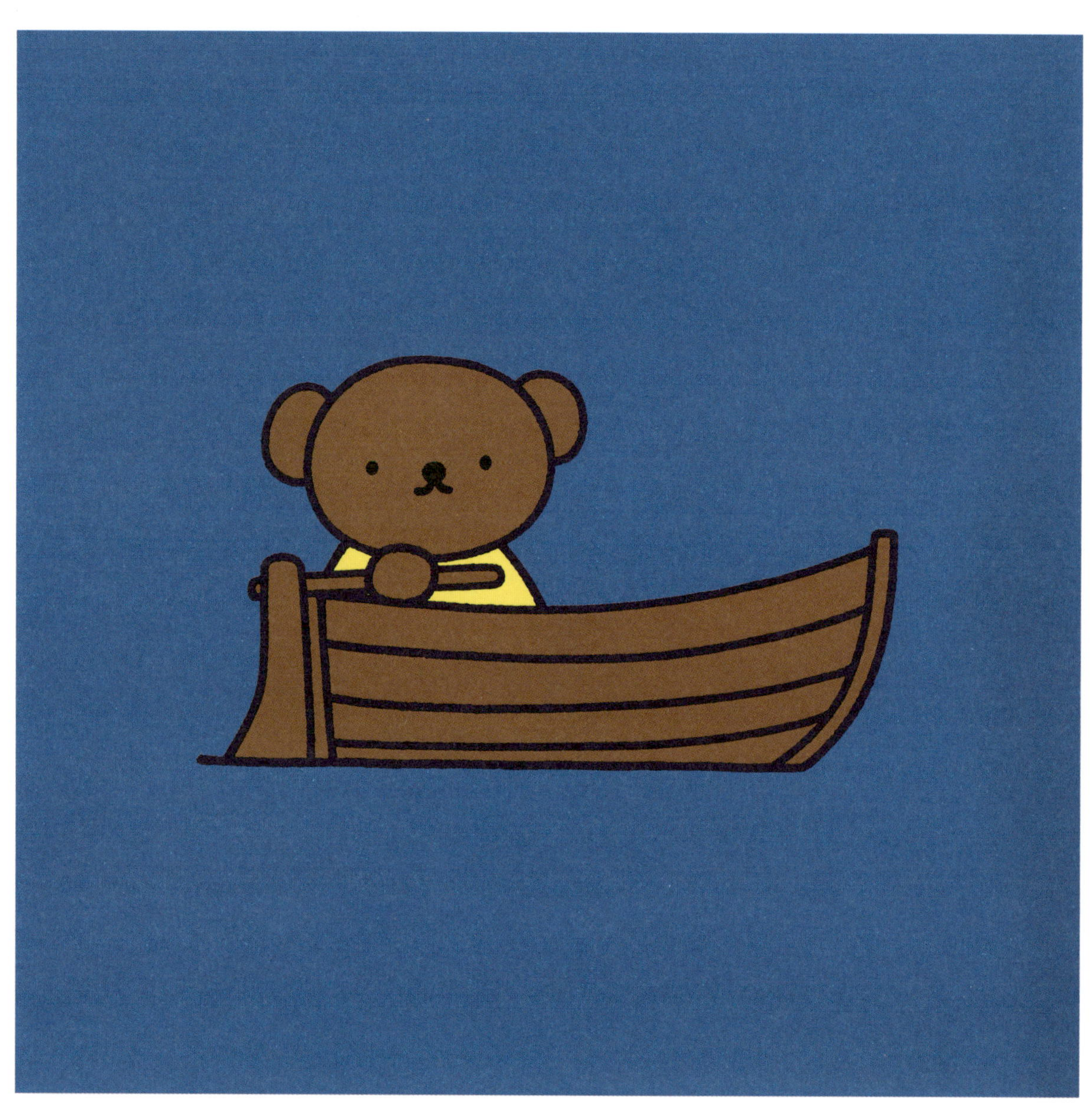

ABOVE

From *Boris Bear's Boat*, 1996

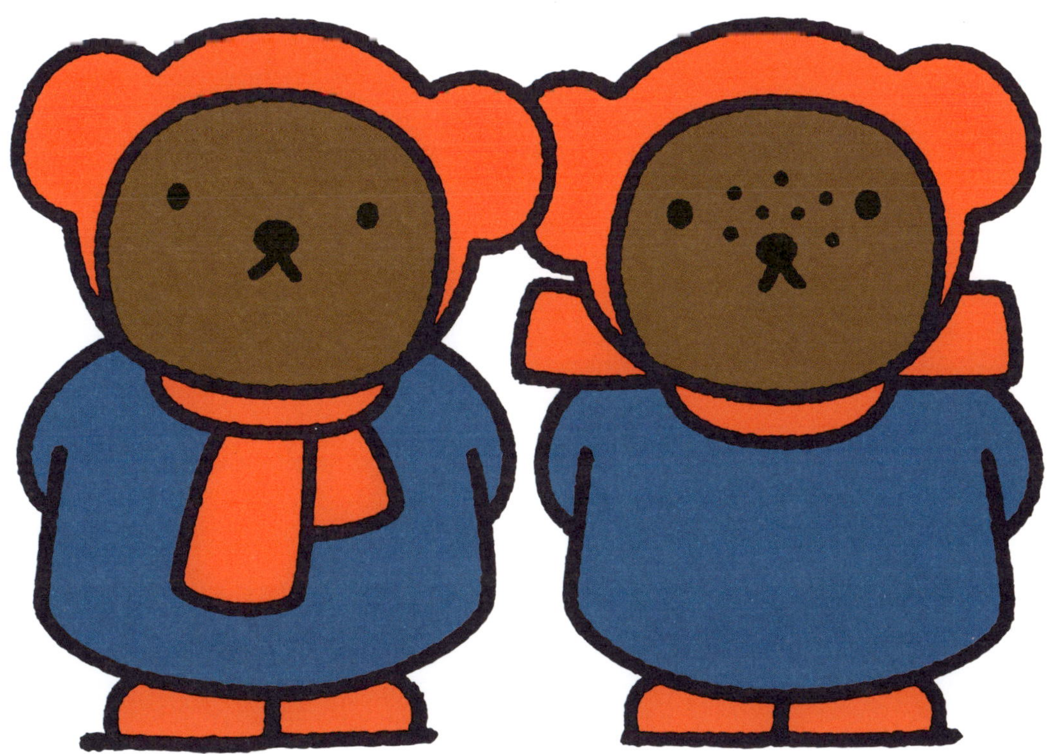

From *Boris in the Snow*, 1994

Meanwhile, Miffy was getting herself noticed. Children loved the little rabbit with her familiar everyday experiences. Bruna didn't abandon his other characters and ideas for books but the shy man now had to face the public. There were school visits, interviews, world tours, fan mail to answer, and hours and hours of signing sessions. The signature was now all onc word: DickBruna. The distillation was complete.

There have been major exhibitions of Bruna's work over the years from Tokyo to Paris, and in 2015, the Rijksmuseum organized a retrospective devoted to sixty years of Bruna's art and graphic designs, placing him in an art-historical context. As Taco Dibbits, General Director of the Rijksmuseum since 2016, said, 'You see that he's part of a tradition going from Saenredam through Vermeer to Mondrian.'[43]

The studio life of the artist

Bruna loved windows, the symbolism and the reality
of them, from his wartime window seat to Matisse's
stained-glass windows to the many windows in his books
and prints. 'Windows have always fascinated me, because
they provide a framework and offer a view. From a point
of seclusion the outside world comes in; by looking outside
through the window this outside world enters more easily.'[44]
The square books are like windows into the world of his
characters and bring comfort and happiness to their readers.

For the onlooker, it is Bruna's studio that offers a window
into his life and work; visitors to the studio today will
still feel his presence. During the course of his life, Bruna
occupied three studios in Utrecht; the attic above the
publishing house, which he left in 1970, 15 Nieuwegracht
and 3 Jeruzalemstraat where he moved in 1981. This is

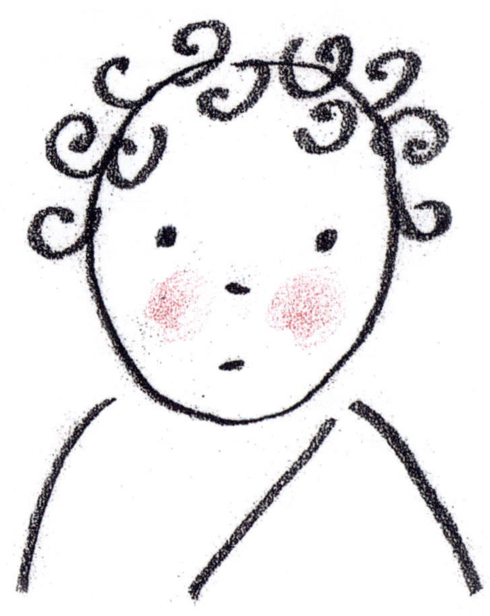

Drawings for Irene left on the
kitchen table

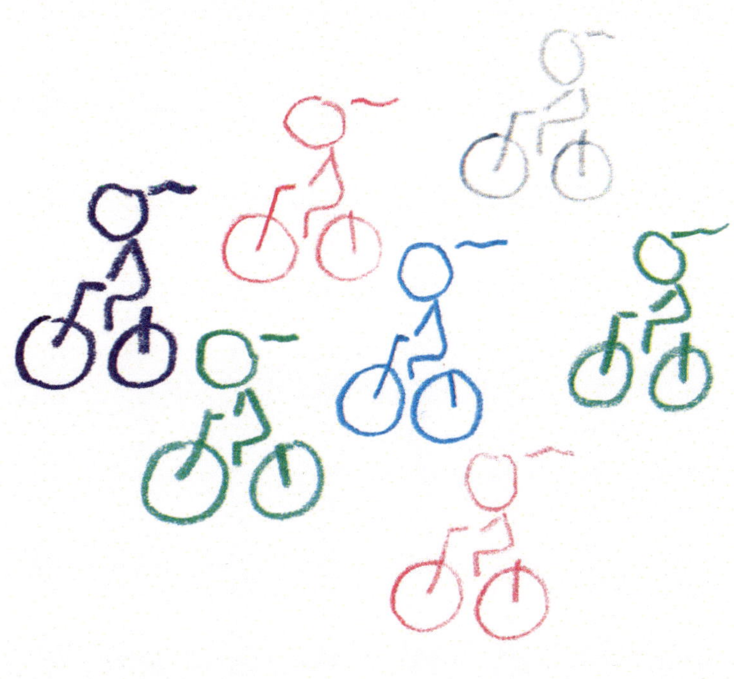

the one that has been meticulously transported to the top
of the Centraal Museum in Utrecht.

Apart from his family, studio life was his life. He was
there six, often seven days a week. Every morning he
would get up around 5.30, squeeze a glass of orange juice
for Irene, and make a little drawing for her to look at over
breakfast, something relevant to her day or something
that had happened the previous day. Irene has kept all
of these drawings.

The children would still be asleep in their bedrooms, each
painted in their favourite colour: Sierk, green; Marc, blue
and Madelon, red.[45]

He would then set off on his bicycle: 'For me, happiness is
cycling to my studio very early in the morning.'[46] For almost
sixty years he was a familiar sight cycling through the old
cobbled streets, past the Rietveld-designed house, which
brought him so much joy and inspiration, before stopping
off for a coffee to read the newspaper.

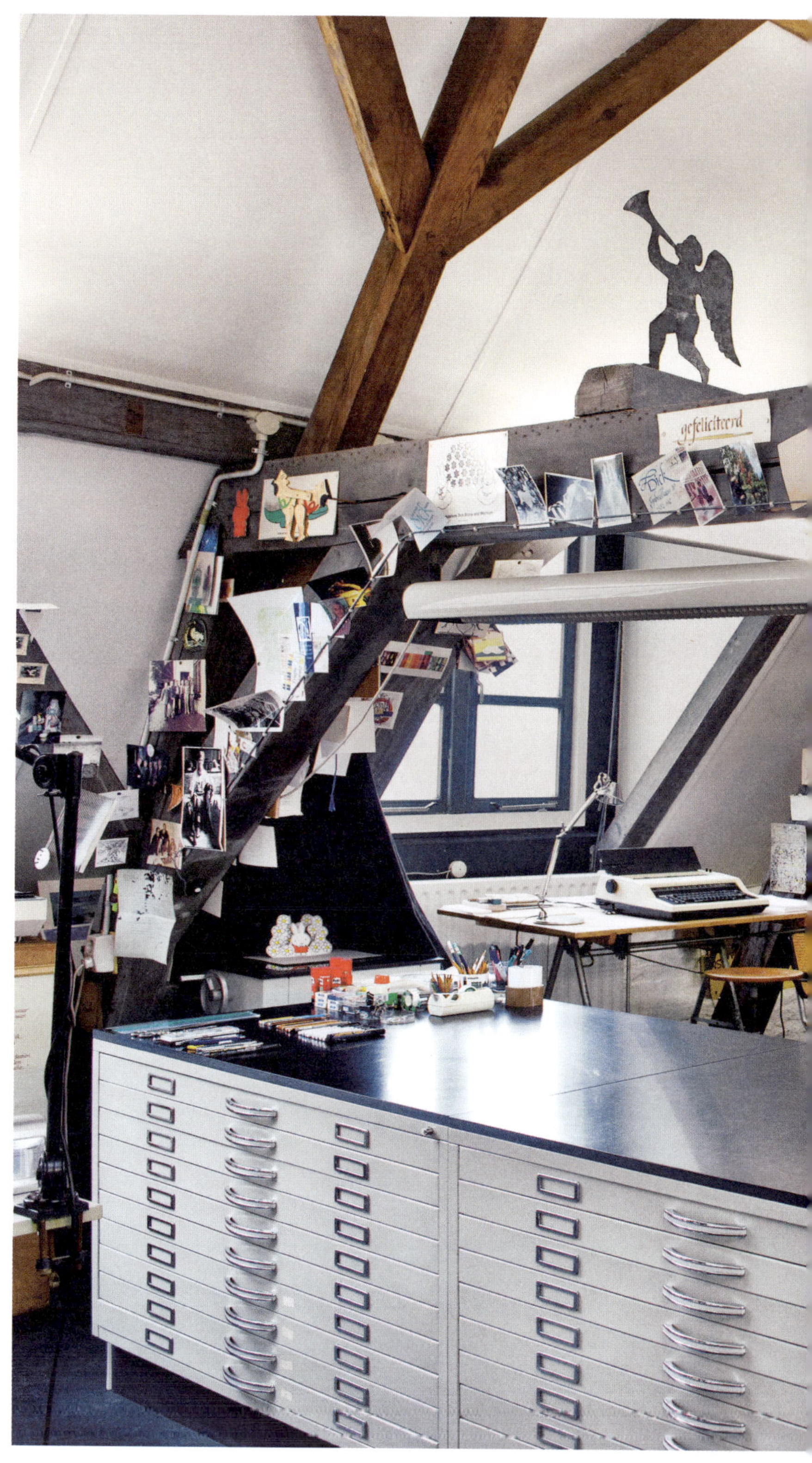

RIGHT
Bruna's studio on Jeruzalemstraat
in Utrecht

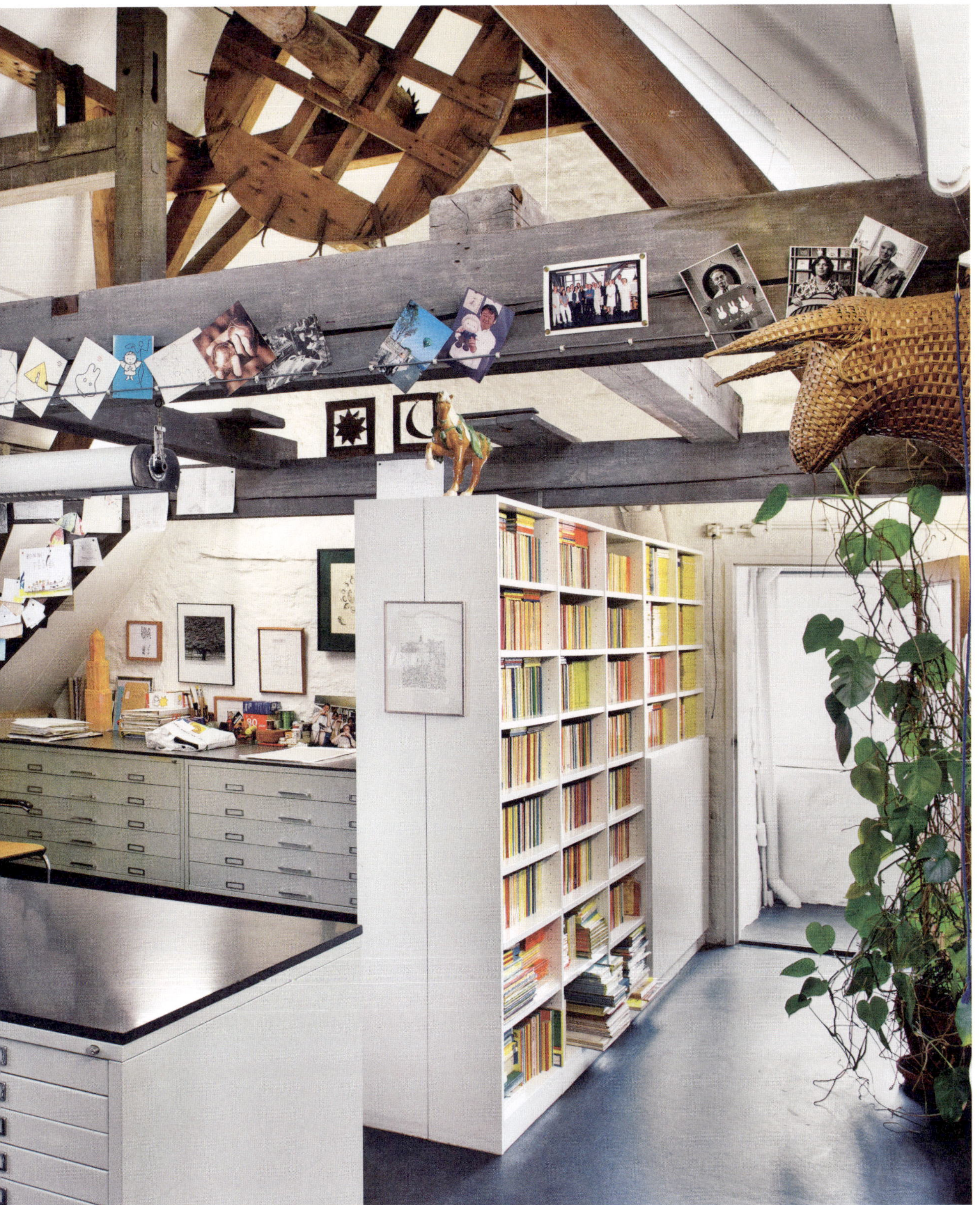

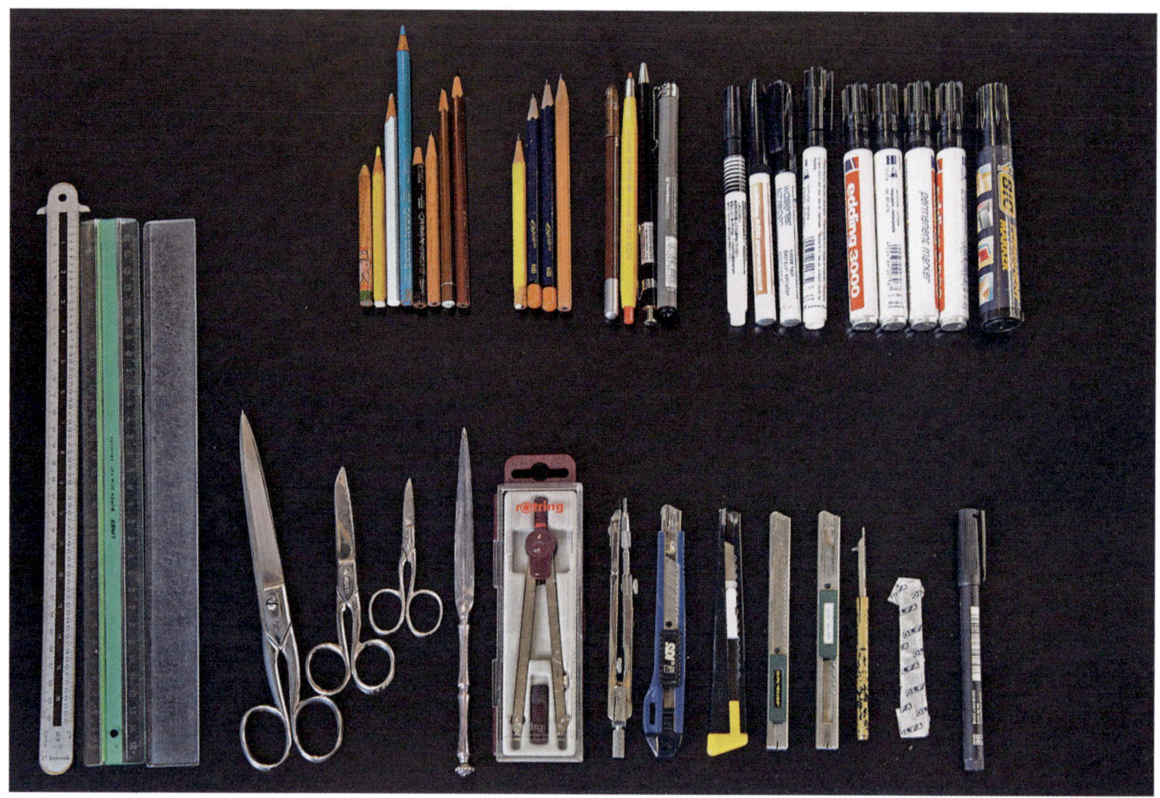

ABOVE
Bruna's desk with art equipment

Then, at his desk, the same nervousness before getting to work. 'Every day I try to do it a little bit better than yesterday.' The mornings were passed drawing and then home for lunch with Irene. On his return to the studio he would occupy the afternoons looking at what he had made earlier, redrawing, revising or not, as necessary. 'I spend a long time making my drawings as simple as possible, throwing lots away, before I reach that moment of recognition.'[47]

While drawing and cutting out, Bruna would listen to his beloved French music but when concentrating on the story the music was switched off so as not to interfere with working out the rhythm. There has been some speculation over the years about Bruna as writer but in the words of Sierk Bruna, 'My father was quite the storyteller.'[48] The illustrations may work as pictograms but the books work as a whole because they have sympathetic accompanying texts to which children can relate. He perfected the illustrations before he wrote the words though always with the narrative

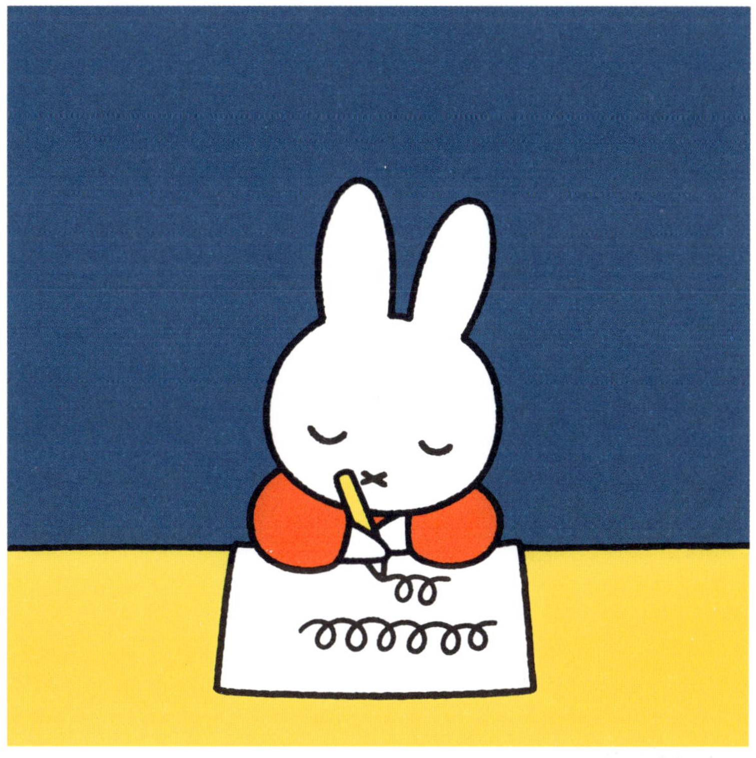

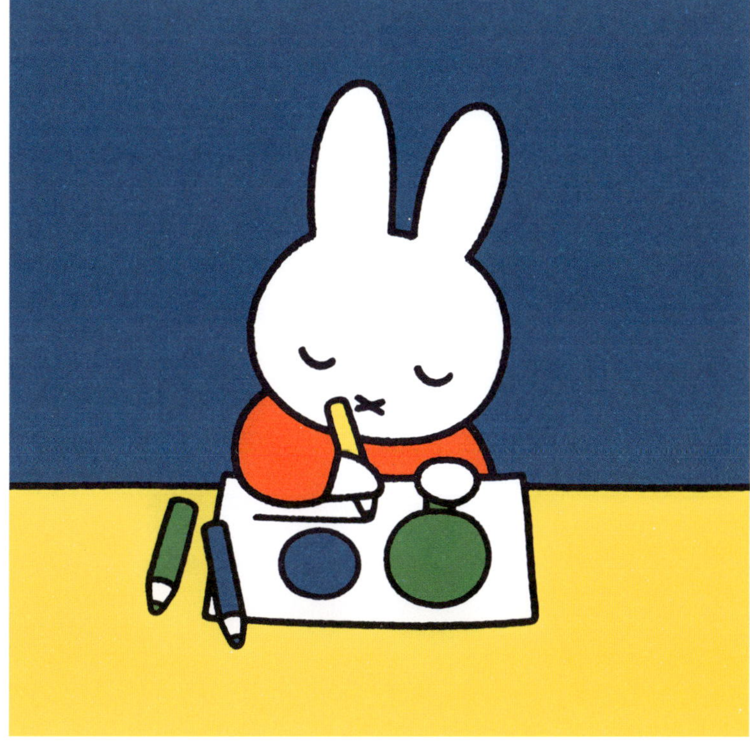

From *Miffy at School*, 1984

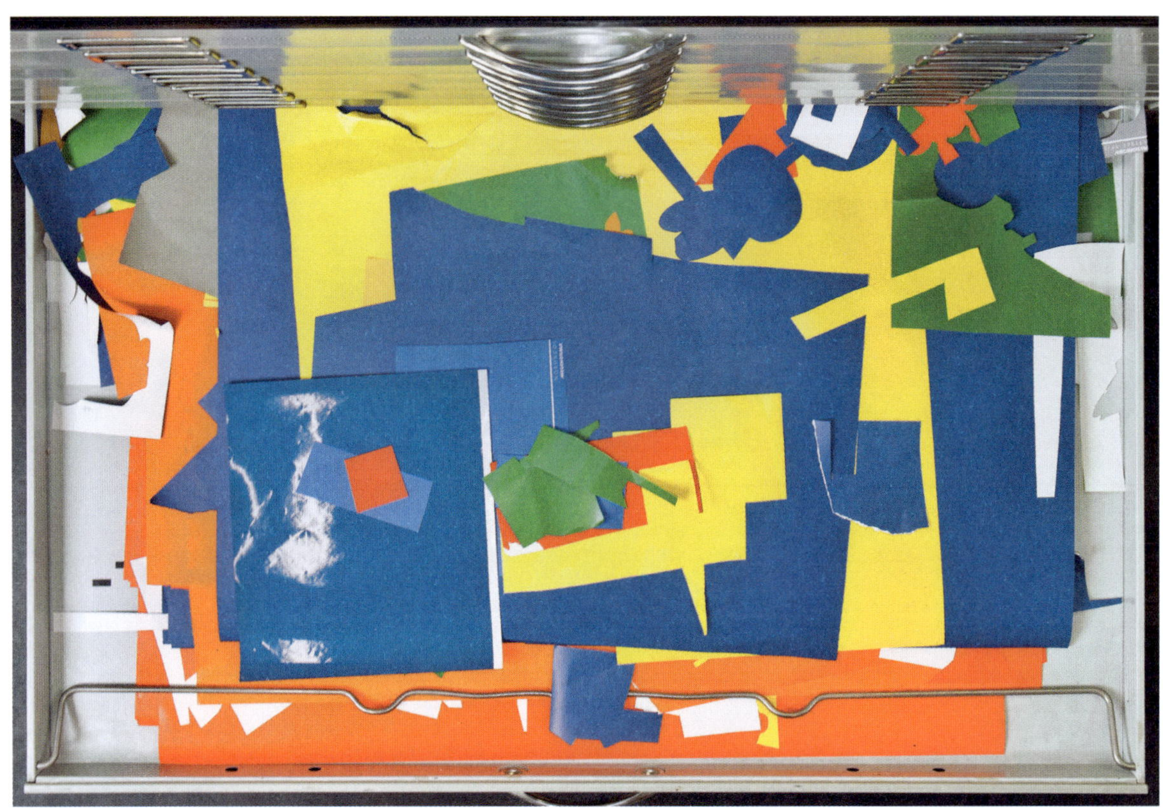

in his head. The result of this, whether intended or not, is that he provided various ways of 'reading' his books.

Bruna went home about five or six in time for dinner with a good glass of wine. 'That's something I like very much.'[49] Then early to bed around nine. No matter how rich or successful he would become, this was the routine Bruna loved. He was 'a stay-at-home'.[50]

If he was nervous about drawing, he got very nervous indeed when it came to showing Irene a new book. 'It is like sitting an exam. I look at her and I can see in her face if it is yes or no.'[51] If the book got a yes, it went through, if not it went in the drawer, perhaps to get a rethink at some point in the future. A look in one of those drawers of his plan chests would reveal more primary-coloured paper for future books than past discarded ones.

The walls of his studio are still covered with letters and drawings from friends and fans. One letter in particular stands out; it is from Charles M. Schulz, the creator of the

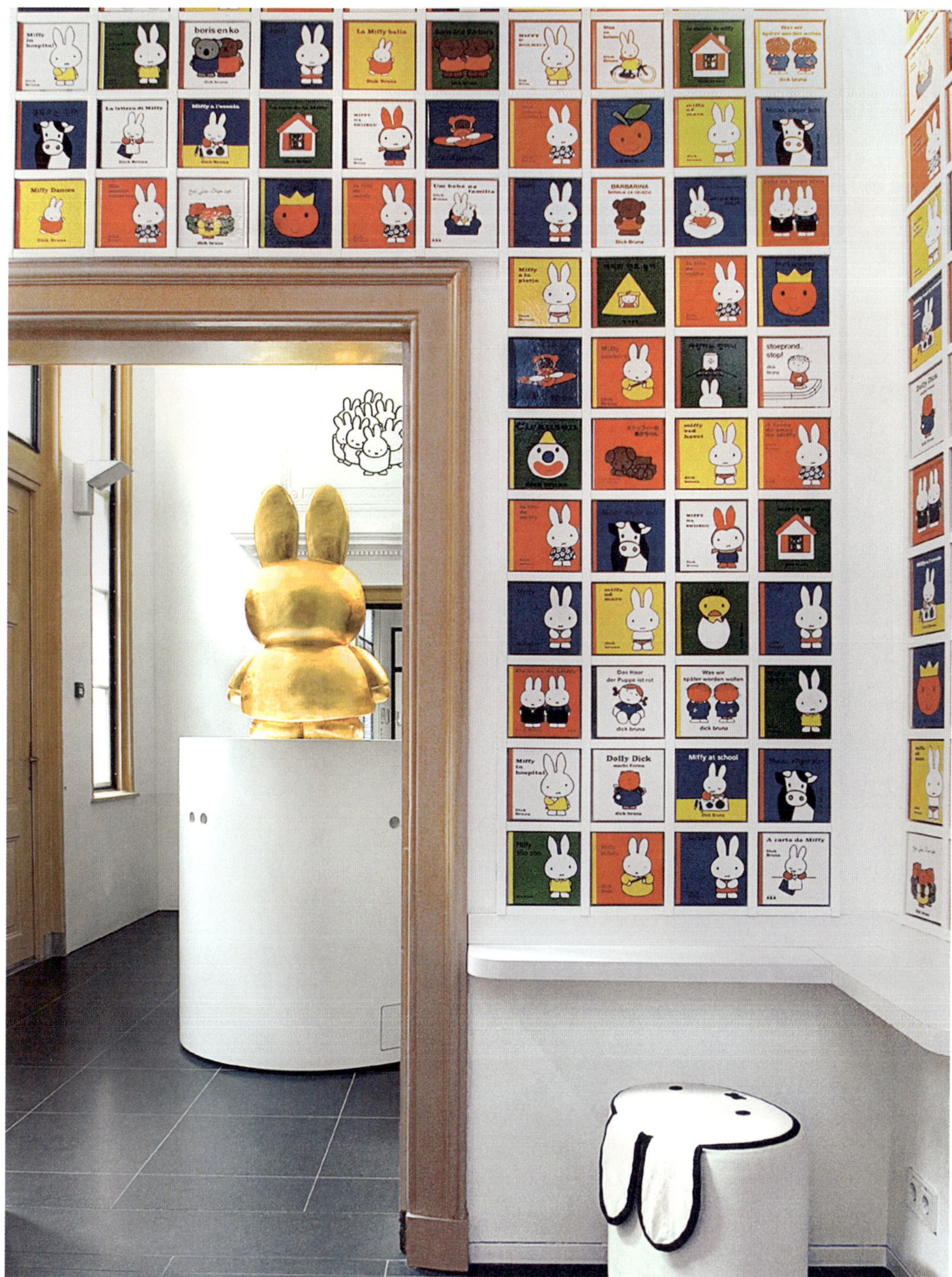

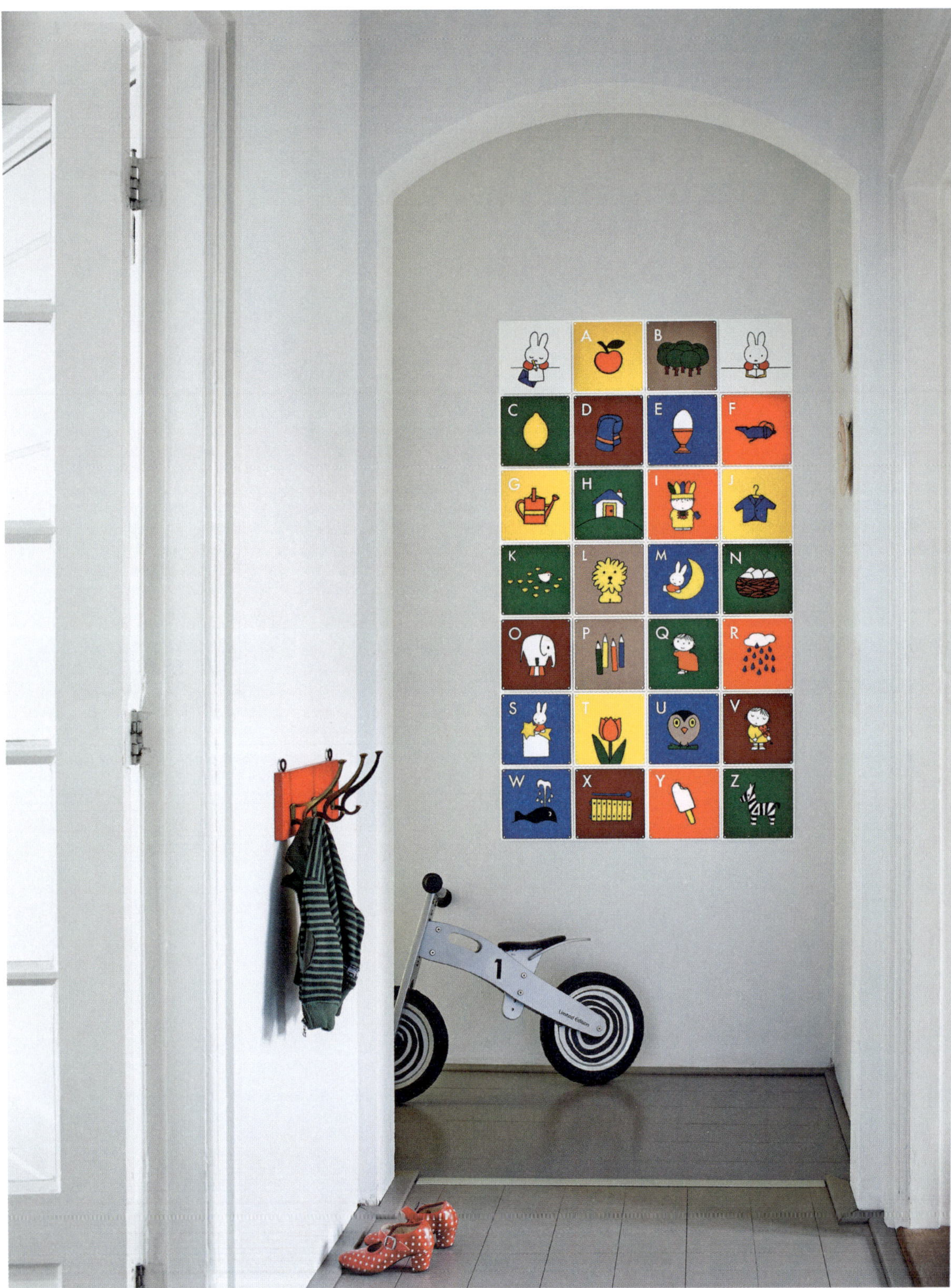

Peanuts comic strip. They met only once but got on well, chatting happily for a couple of hours like old friends, and they became pen friends. Schulz told him how he used one hand to hold the other hand steady to help him draw straight lines. Bruna felt fortunate that he never needed to use the advice to draw his own unique sensitive line.

The shelves are filled with foreign language editions of his books and other children's books including those of Roald Dahl, Ludwig Bemelmans, Tomi Ungerer and John Burningham.

There are many, many presents from Miffy fans around the world. As one would expect, everything is neatly arranged and organized. If visitors came they would get tea and Dutch biscuits. Bruna liked his visitors to be punctual but he was never impolite and his twinkly eyes would never suggest he'd prefer to get back to his desk.

One day, while cycling out on an errand for his summer holiday, Bruna stopped and got off his bicycle. Those who saw him thought nothing of it, accustomed to the artist stopping to make a note of one kind or another. But on this occasion, he had lost his breath. A visit to the doctor confirmed it was more serious and he needed to have a pacemaker fitted. After that, he determined to stop going to

OPPOSITE
Bruna alphabet, wall decoration by IXXI Design, the Netherlands

BELOW
Bruna's children's postage stamps, the Netherlands, 2005

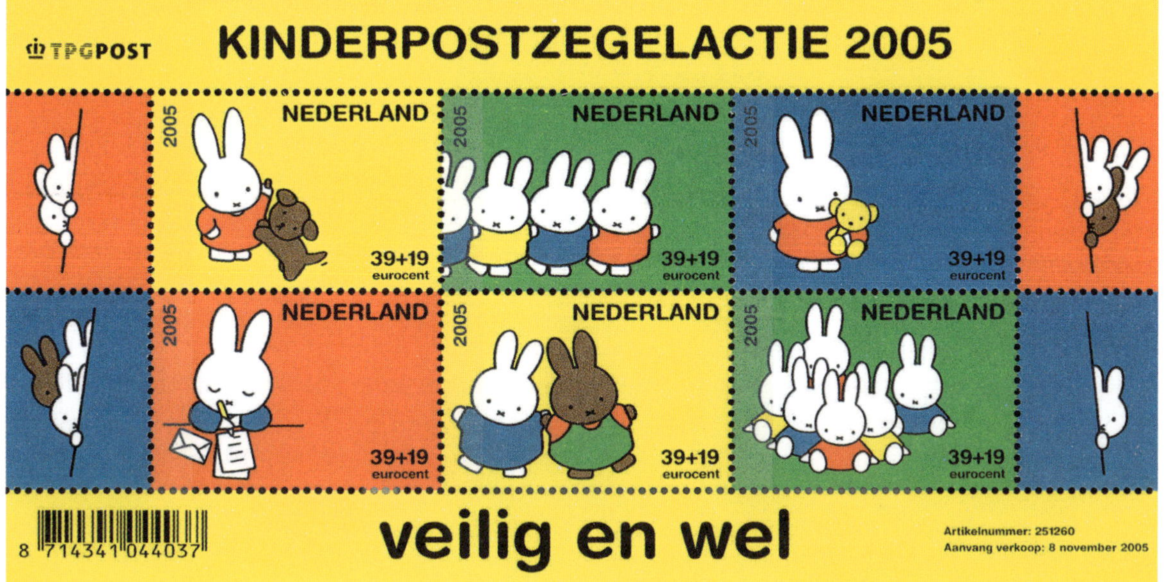

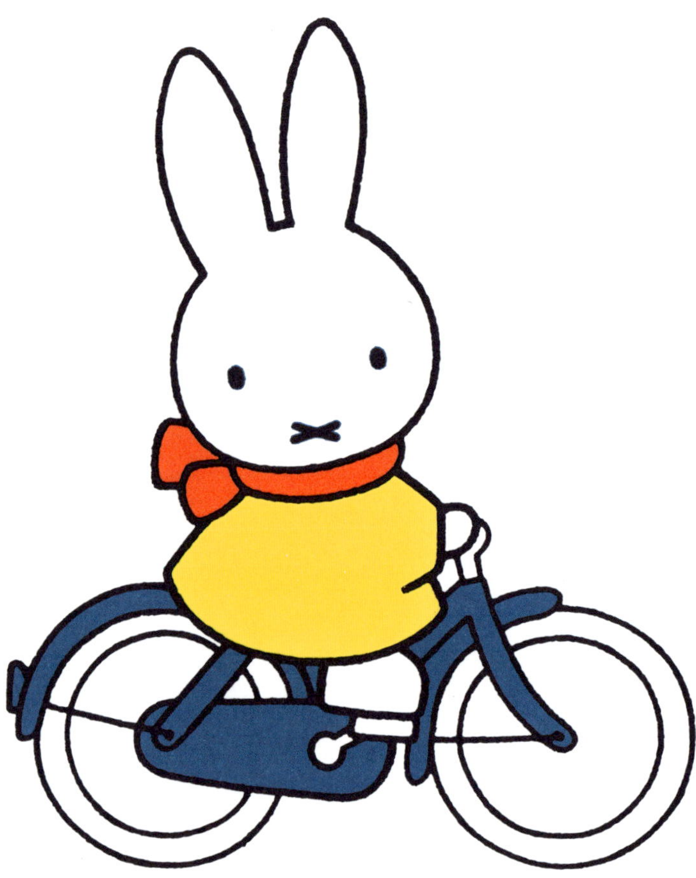

his studio. Despite the cajoling of his family, surprised at his abrupt decision, he would not be persuaded. His mind was made up; he didn't want to work if he couldn't give it his all.

So it was that on a sunny summer's day in 2011, Bruna laid out his perfectly sharpened pencils, pens, paintbrushes and scissors. As usual he left everything set up for the following day. He locked up, got on his bike and went home. He never returned to work at his studio.

Bruna died peacefully in his sleep on 16 February 2017. By the time of his death, he had created 124 picture books, 32 of them featuring Miffy with over 85 million sales across more than 50 languages. The little rabbit had become an industry and Bruna an international star far beyond the sphere of children's books. The simple complexity of his work, the colours, the space, carefully chosen text and the complete control have paradoxically allowed for

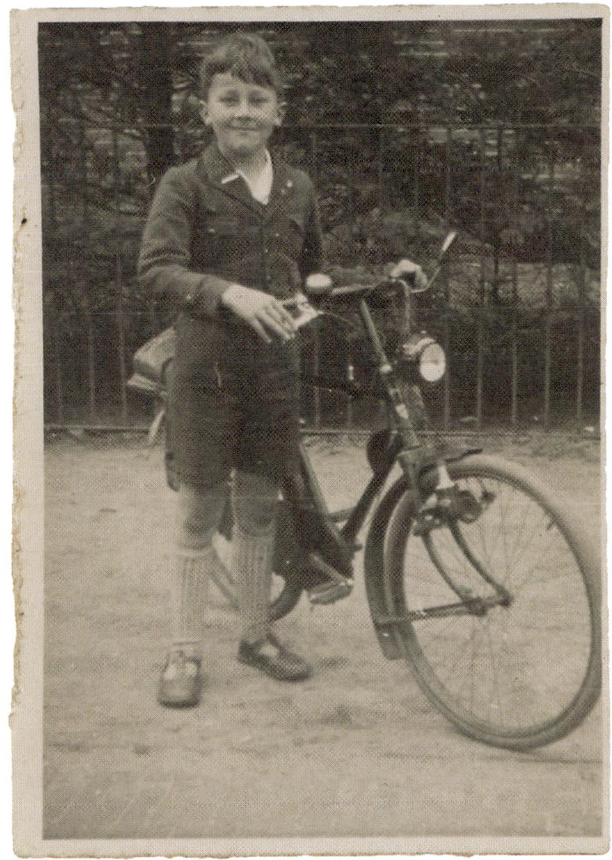

ABOVE
Bruna, 11 years old, Zeist

interpretation and imagination across ages and artistic disciplines. Dick Bruna created a character that speaks to all of us. That is quite an achievement.

When I am finished the drawings are finished.[52]

But this is not the end of the story. The drawings may have finished but the Miffy juggernaut keeps going and Bruna's legacy lives on; the books continue to sell in the millions. There are films, musicals, exhibitions and merchandising in all primary-coloured shapes and sizes.

In 2006, the Bruna Huis opened in Utrecht facing the Centraal Museum. Following a renovation programme, it reopened in 2016 as the Miffy Museum with more than 1,200 works on permanent display. It is a wonderland for Miffy-loving kids and a polestar for Bruna fans.

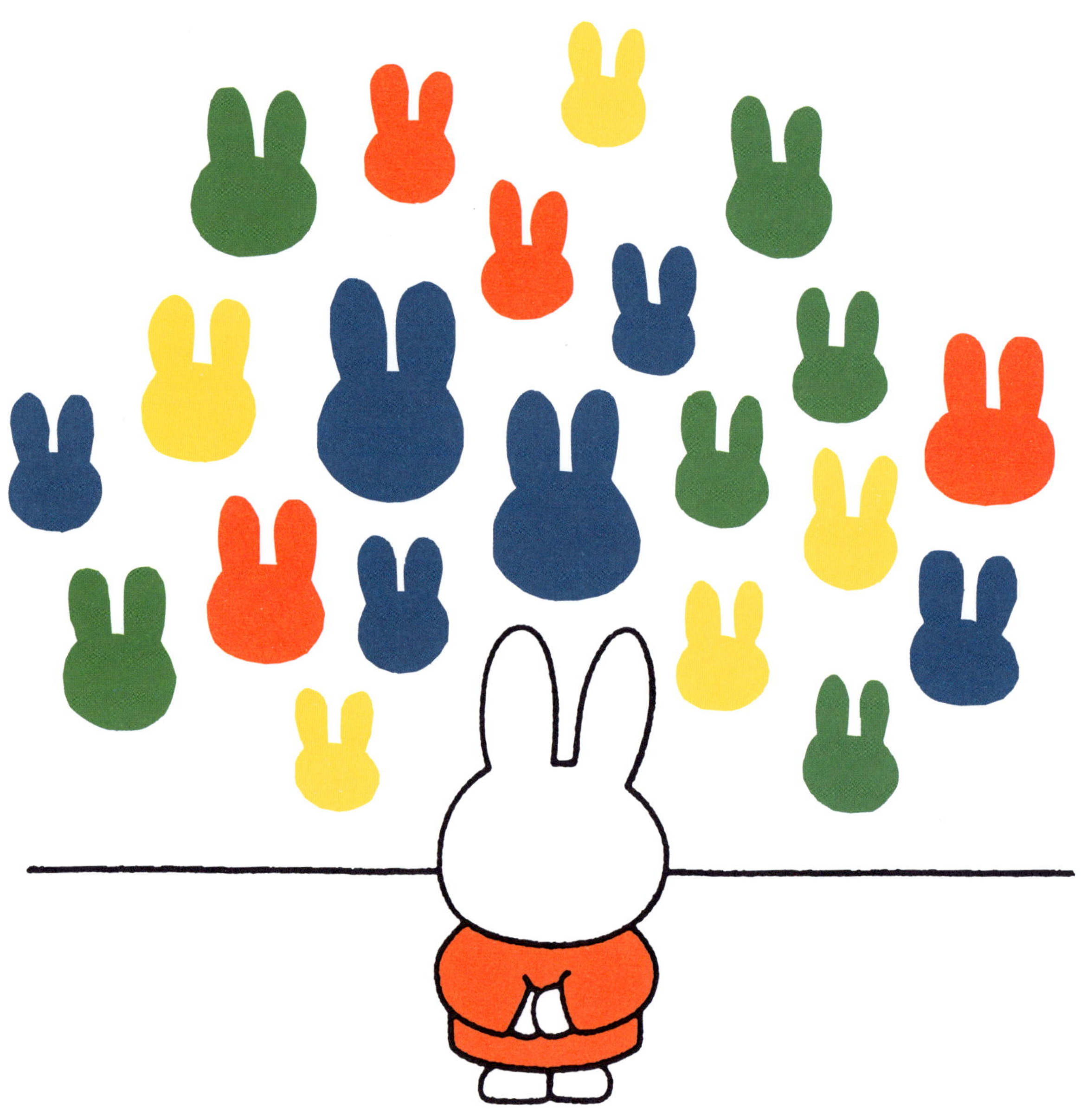

ABOVE
From *Miffy at the Gallery*, 1997

If Bruna had designed the cover of his own life story, what cut-out silhouette might he have chosen? A bicycle? Scissors and finely trimmed paintbrush, beautifully cut out and placed onto a square window format? Might he have added a fluffy moustache? Would the logo be a rabbit or a bear? Although this cover doesn't exist, *Miffy at the Gallery*, published in 1997, is like a memoir in twelve spreads, revealing not only Bruna's influences but also his playfulness and lifelong love of art. In one image, *Matisse's Sheaf*, one of Bruna's favourite works of art has been reproduced using the heads of rabbits that are unmistakeably Miffy. As we look at the rare view of the back of Miffy's head gazing up at the painting, we don't need to see the two dots and a cross to discern the joy and wonder on her face. This illustration tells us all we need to know about Dick Bruna, the artist.

BELOW
Dick Bruna, 2010

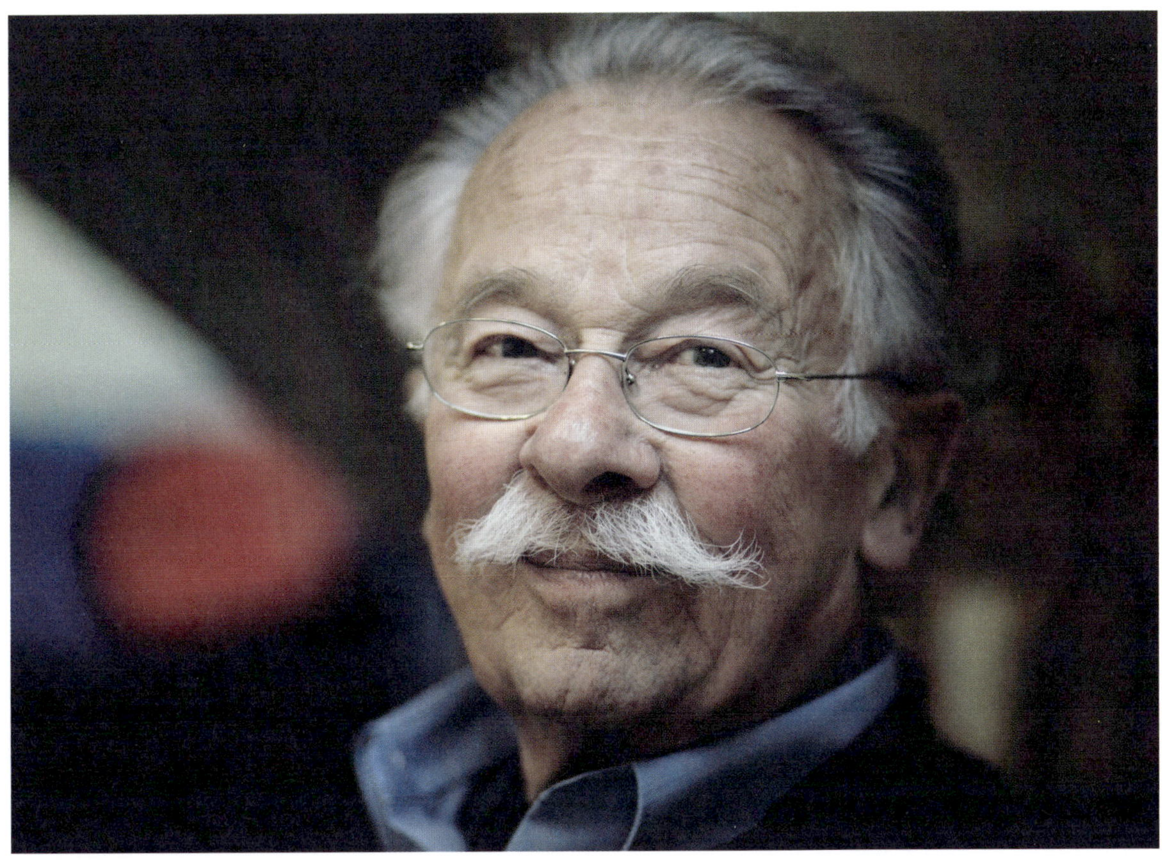

NOTES

1. Lisa Allardice, 'Bunny love', *The Guardian*, 15 February 2006.
2. Ella Reitsma and Kees Nieuwenhuijzen, *Paradise in Pictograms: The Work of Dick Bruna*, Mercis bv, 1991, p. 12.
3. *Simply Bruna* (documentary), AVRO – Wereldomroep – Cine/Vista, 1995
4. Joke Linders, Koosje Sierman, Ivo de Wijs, Truusje Vrooland-Löb, *Dick Bruna*, Waanders Publishers, Zwolle/Mercis bv, 2006, p. 73.
5. Horatia Harrod, *The Telegraph*, 31 July 2008.
6. Benjamin Secher, 'I saw Matisse – and came up with Miffy', *The Telegraph*, 9 December 2006.
7. Reitsma, *Paradise in Pictograms*, op. cit., p. 16.
8. Linders et al., *Dick Bruna*, op. cit., p. 97.
9. Reitsma, *Paradise in Pictograms*, op. cit., p. 18.
10. Horatia Harrod, *The Telegraph*, 31 July 2008.
11. Benjamin Secher, *The Telegraph*, 9 December 2006.
12. Caro Verbeek, *Dick Bruna. Artist*, published to accompany the exhibition *Dick Bruna. Artist*, Rijksmuseum, Amsterdam, 27 August – 15 November 2015, p. 56.
13. Ibid., p. 27.
14. Alastair Sooke, *The Telegraph*, 27 April 2010.
15. Alastair Sooke, *Henri Matisse: A Second Life*, quoted in Alastair Sooke, 'How Henri Matisse created his masterpiece', *The Telegraph*, 15 April 2014.
16. *Simply Bruna* (documentary), op. cit.
17. Lucy Davies, 'Many hoppy returns: Miffy turns 60', *The Telegraph*, 20 June 2015.
18. Reitsma, *Paradise in Pictograms*, op. cit., p. 32.
19. *Simply Bruna* (documentary), op. cit.
20. Céline Rutten, *Gesprekken met Dick Bruna*, Atlas, Amsterdam, 2011.
21. Reitsma, *Paradise in Pictograms*, op. cit., p. 48.
22. Linders et al., *Dick Bruna*, op. cit., p. 407.
23. Ibid., p. 400.
24. Reitsma, *Paradise in Pictograms*, op. cit., p. 48.
25. Linders et al., *Dick Bruna*, op. cit., p. 325.
26. Simenon letter, Bruna private collection, Mercis bv.
27. Reitsma, *Paradise in Pictograms*, op. cit., p. 48.
28. Ibid., p. 28.
29. Douglas Martin, *The New York Times*, 1 November 2002.
30. Reitsma, *Paradise in Pictograms*, op. cit., p. 54.
31. *Simply Bruna* (documentary), op. cit.
32. Dick Bruna, *Miffy at the Seaside*, translated by Patricia Crampton, World International, 1997.
33. Reitsma, *Paradise in Pictograms*, op. cit., p. 56.
34. Ibid.
35. Linders et al., *Dick Bruna*, op. cit., p. 38.
36. Benjamin Secher, *The Telegraph*, 9 December 2006.
37. Karin van Zwieten (ed.), *60 Years of Miffy, A Celebration of Miffy's 60th Anniversary*, Mercis bv, 2015.
38. *Icon and Inspiration*, Human Factor Television, commissioned by Mercis bv, 2005.
39. Horatia Harrod, *The Telegraph*, 31 July 2008.
40. Linders et al., *Dick Bruna*, op. cit., p. 408.
41. Ibid., p. 292.
42. Ibid., p. 276.
43. Taco Dibbits, *The New York Times*, 20 February 2017.
44. Linders et al., *Dick Bruna*, op. cit., p. 221.
45. Lucy Davies, *The Telegraph*, 20 June 2015.
46. Miffy.com, copyright Mercis bv.
47. Nina Siegal, *The New York Times*, 20 February 2017.
48. Lucy Davies, *The Telegraph*, 20 June 2015.
49. Lisa Allardice, *The Guardian*, 15 February 2006.
50. Reitsma, *Paradise in Pictograms*, op. cit., p. 72.
51. Lisa Allardice, *The Guardian*, 15 February 2006.
52. Benjamin Secher, *The Telegraph*, 9 December 2006.

SELECT BIBLIOGRAPHY

Books written and illustrated by Dick Bruna

Titles are as they appear on the Dutch edition (with English translation) and the year is that of first publication in the Netherlands. English editions of the books do not always exist and sometimes have different titles.

de appel (The apple), 1953 (second version, 1959)
toto in volendam, 1955
nijntje (Miffy), 1955 (second version, 1963)
nijntje in de dierentuin (Miffy at the zoo), 1955 (second version, 1963)

kleine koning (The small king), 1955
tijs, 1957
de auto (The car), 1957
het vogeltje (The bird), 1959
poesje nel (Kitty Nell), 1959
fien en pien (Tilly and Tessa), 1959
het ei (The egg), 1962
de koning (The king), 1962
circus, 1962
de vis (The fish), 1962
nijntje in de sneeuw (Miffy in the snow), 1963
nijntje aan zee (Miffy at the seaside), 1963

kerstmis (Christmas), 1963
de school (The school), 1964
de matroos (The sailor), 1964
ik kan lezen (I can read), 1969
ik kan nog meer lezen (I can read more), 1969
assepoester (Cinderella), 1966
klein duimpje (Hop-O'-My-Thumb), 1966
roodkapje (Red Riding Hood), 1966
sneeuwwitje (Snow White), 1966
b is een beer (B is for bear), 1967
boek zonder woorden (A story to tell), 1968
telboek (I can count), 1968

snuffie (Snuffy), 1969

snuffie en de brand (Snuffy and the fire), 1969

nijntje vliegt (Miffy goes flying), 1970

het feest van nijntje (Miffy's birthday), 1970

telboek 2 (I can count more), 1972

mijn hemd is wit (My vest is white), 1972

dierenboek (Animal book), 1972

dieren uit ons land (Animals from our land), 1972

dieren uit andere landen (Animals from other countries), 1972

boek zonder woorden 2 (Another story to tell), 1974

ik ben een clown (I am a Clown), 1974

bloemenboek (Flower book), 1975

nijntje in de speeltuin (Miffy at the playground), 1975

nijntje in het ziekenhuis (Miffy in hospital), 1975

ik kan nog veel meer lezen (I can read much more), 1976

ik kan moeilijke woorden lezen (I can read difficult words), 1976

basje gaat logeren bij kinderneurologie (Basje goes to stay at the children's neurology department), 1977

betje big (Poppy Pig), 1977

de tuin van betje big (Poppy Pig's garden), 1977

verjaardagboekje t.b.v. UNICEF (Birthday book), 1979

nijntjes droom (Miffy's dream), 1979

betje big gaat naar de markt (Poppy Pig goes to market), 1980

heb jij een hobbie? (When I grow up), 1980

ik kan sommen maken (I can do sums), 1980

ik kan nog meer sommen maken (I can do more sums), 1980

jeroen heeft hemofilie (Children's haemophilia book), 1980

rond, vierkant, driehoekig (Round, square, triangular), 1982

jan (Farmer John), 1982

nijntje op de fiets (Miffy's bicycle), 1982

de redding (The rescue), 1984

wij hebben een orkest (The orchestra), 1984

nijntje op school (Miffy at school), 1984

sportboek (My book of sports), 1985

wie zijn hoed is dat? (Whose hat is that?) 1985

wie zijn rug is dat? (Back to front), 1985

lente, zomer, herfst en winter (Spring, summer, autumn, winter), 1986

de verjaardag van betje big (Poppy Pig's birthday), 1986

de puppies van snuffie (Snuffy's puppies), 1986

nijntje gaat logeren (Miffy goes to stay), 1988

opa and oma pluis (Grandpa and Grandma Bunny), 1988

stoeprand...stop! (Stop at the kerb!), 1988

iris een boek zonder woorden (Iris a book without words), 1988 (revised edition, 2000)

boris beer (Boris Bear), 1989

boris en barbara (Boris and Barbara), 1989

boris op de berg (Boris on the mountain), 1989

de schrijfster (The authoress), 1990

lotje (Lottie), 1990

nijntje huilt (Miffy is crying), 1991

het huis van nijntje (Miffy's house), 1991

het feest van tante trijn (Auntie Alice's party), 1992

boris in de sneeuw (Boris in the snow), 1994

boris, barbara en basje (Boris, Barbara and Benny), 1994

betje big is ziek (Poppy Pig is sick), 1994

eegje egel (Hettie Hedgehog), 1995

boe zegt de koe (Moo says the cow), 1995

nijntje in de tent (Miffy in the tent), 1995

wat wij later worden (What we're going to be), 1996

het haar van de pop is rood (The dolly's hair is red), 1996

de boot van boris (Boris Bear's boat), 1996

lieve oma pluis (Dear Grandma Bunny), 1996

weet jij waarom ik huil? (Do you know why I am crying?), 1997

nijntje in het museum (Miffy at the gallery), 1997

betje big gaat met vakantie (Poppy Pig goes on holiday), 1998

betje big gaat met vakantie (Poppy Pig's shop), 1998

ruben en de ark van noach (Caleb and Noah's ark), 1998

nijntje en nina (Miffy and Melanie), 1999

pim en wim (Ping and Bing), 1999

boris en de paraplu (Boris and the umbrella), 1999

meneer knie (Mister Knee), 2000

het spook nijntje (Miffy the ghost), 2001

nijntje de toverfee (Miffy the fairy), 2001

nijntje danst (Miffy dances), 2002

boris de piloot (Boris the pilot), 2002

de verkleedkist van barbara (Barbara's clothes chest), 2002

boris de kampioen (Boris the champion), 2003

de brief van nijntje (Miffy's letter), 2003

kleine pluis (The new baby), 2003

een lied voor betje big (A song for Poppy Pig), 2004

de tuin van nijntje (Miffy's garden), 2004

snuffie is zoek (Snuffy is missing), 2005

boris en ko (Boris and Ko), 2005

nijntje in luilekkerland (Miffy in lolly land), 2005

boris doet de boodschappen (Boris does the shopping), 2005

een fluit voor nijntje (A flute for Miffy), 2005

vogel piet (Peter Bird), 2006

hangoor (Flopear), 2006

koningin nijntje (Queen Miffy), 2007

een maatje voor snuffie (A friend for Snuffy), 2008

nijntje is stout (Miffy is naughty), 2008

een cadeau voor opa pluis (A present for Grandpa Bunny), 2009

knorretje (Grunty), 2010

op de step (On my scooter), 2010

knorretje en de oren van nijntje (Grunty Pig and Miffy's ears), 2011

ezelsoor (Donkey's ear), 2012

Books and articles about Dick Bruna

Allardice, Lisa, 'Bunny love', *The Guardian*, 15 February 2006

Harrod, Horatia, 'Dick Bruna talks about his life and work', *The Telegraph*, 31 July 2008

Kohnstamm, Dolf, *The Extra in the Ordinary: Children's Books by Dick Bruna*, Mercis bv, 1976

Linders, Joke, Koosje Sierman, Ivo de Wijs and Truusje Vrooland-Löb, *Dick Bruna*, Waanders Publishers, Zwolle/ Mercis Publishing bv, Amsterdam, 2006

Reitsma, Ella and Kees Nieuwenhuijzen, *Paradise in Pictograms: The Work of Dick Bruna*, commissioned by Mercis bv, Amsterdam, 1991

Secher, Benjamin, 'I saw Matisse – and came up with Miffy', *The Telegraph*, 9 December 2006

Verbeek, Caro, *Dick Bruna. Artist*, published to accompany the exhibition *Dick Bruna. Artist*, Rijksmuseum, Amsterdam, 27 August – 15 November 2015

Zwieten, Karin van (ed.), *60 Years of Miffy, A Celebration of Miffy's 60th Anniversary*, Mercis bv, 2015

1927 Dick Bruna born in Utrecht

1943 Writes his first book, *Japie*

1946 Designs first book cover for his father's publishing company, A. W. Bruna & Zoon Uitgevers

1947 Designs his first poster

1952 Employed by A. W. Bruna as a book cover and poster designer

1953 Publishes his first picture book, *The Apple*. Marries Irene de Jongh

1954 Birth of son Sierk

1955 The first Miffy book published in rectangular format

1956 Designs first poster for the *Zwarte Beertjes* series

1958 Birth of son Marc. Receives Afficheprijs for a *Zwarte Beertjes* poster

1959 Introduction of the distinctive square format (15.5 x 15.5 cm) for his books

1961 Birth of daughter Madelon

1963 A new edition of *Miffy* published in square format. Miffy launched in the UK by Methuen

1964 Miffy books published in Japan with sixteen reprints within four years

1969 Designs a series of five postage stamps for the PTT postal company in the Netherlands

1971 Mercis bv established. Start of merchandising with the production of jigsaw puzzles by Ravensburger

1972 Produces murals for the children's ward of a new hospital in Leidschendam, the Netherlands

1975 Designs greetings cards for Amnesty International

1977 Municipal Museum in Arnhem hosts a Miffy exhibition; Bruna is presented as a museum artist for the first time

1980 Commissioned by the Royal Victoria Infirmary, Newcastle upon Tyne, to produce *The Children's Haemophilia Book*, a storybook to highlight the dangers of this condition

1983 Decorated as a Knight of the Order of Orange-Nassau in the Netherlands

1986 Designs the symbol 'Utrecht – a city after my own heart', which is still in use

1987 Presented with the official Lapel Pin of the City of Utrecht to honour his 60th birthday

1990 Presented with the Golden Brush Award for the illustrations in *Boris Bear*. Receives D. A.

Thiemeprijs for his entire *oeuvre*

1991 Retrospective at the Georges Pompidou Centre in Paris. *Miffy at the Seaside* is published in Braille for the first time (in Dutch and English) to mark the 20th anniversary of Mercis bv

1992 Dutch television première of fifty-two short films based on the stories in the books

1994 A bronze statue of Miffy created by his son Marc is erected in Utrecht

1995 Designs Christmas postage stamps and related products for the Royal PTT postal company. Receives H. N. Werkmanprijs for his cover and poster designs. Mercis Publishing bv established

1996 Retrospective, *The Smell of Success*, Groninger Museum. Opening of first Miffy shop in Amsterdam. Wins the Silver Brush Award for the illustrations in *Miffy in the Tent*

1997 Becomes first non-national to design a series of postage stamps for the Japanese Ministry of Post. Wins Silver Slate Award for the text of *Dear Grandma Bunny*

1999 Exhibition *The World of Dick Bruna* tours Japan for two years as part of the 400th anniversary of trading relations between the Netherlands and Japan, attracting 370,000 visitors

2000 Miffy listed in the *Guinness Book of Records* for receiving a record number of birthday cards (37,865 from more than eighty countries). Retrospective exhibition in the Centraal Museum in Utrecht. Creates the book *Donkey's Ear* at the request of the Foundation for the Promotion of Dutch Books (CPNB)

2001 Première of *Miffy the Musical*. Publication of his hundredth children's book. Decorated as Knight Commander in the Order of the Lion of the Netherlands, the highest honour that can be bestowed on a civilian in the Netherlands

2002 Designs the logo for World AIDS Day as part of the 'Stop AIDS Now' campaign

2003 Interactive exhibition at The Crayola FACTORY® children's museum in the USA

2004 Great Ormond Street Hospital, London, creates a Miffy Ward, its first ever character-themed

ward. Miffy appointed as New York City's Family Tourism Ambassador, to attract tourist families back to the city post 9/11

2005 The first Miffy coin is struck at the Royal Dutch Mint

2006 Dick Bruna House (part of the Centraal Museum) opens in Utrecht, with a permanent exhibition of 1,200 original works. *Dutch Treats: Contemporary Illustrations from the Netherlands* at the Eric Carle Museum in the USA features the work of thirteen artists including Bruna. UK touring exhibition *Happy Birthday Miffy!* opens in London as the inaugural exhibition for the reopening of the V&A Museum of Childhood. *dick bruna – a biography* is published by Waanders in both Dutch and English

2007 Celebrates his 80th birthday. Designs a special illustration for UNICEF. Receives a special Golden Lapel Pin of the City of Utrecht

2008 Designs a *Zwarte Beertjes* cover for the first time in forty years to mark the 140th anniversary of A. W. Bruna. Included in Andrew Zuckerman's *Wisdom* project featuring seventy-five of the world's most eminent elders of varying disciplines

2010 Photographed by Erwin Olaf for *A Journey to Excellence*, a tribute to Dutch citizens who are among the best in their field, now part of the permanent collection in the Rijksmuseum

2011 Selection of 120 works given on long-term loan to the Print Room at the Rijksmuseum. *Miffy in Fashion* exhibition at Centraal Museum. Retires in the summer. Miffy becomes the symbol for the international Children's Museum Award, its trophy a scale model of the bronze Miffy statue in Utrecht

2013 *Miffy the Movie* opens in the Netherlands, breaking box office records for a film aimed at very young children

2014 The first indoor Miffy theme park opens in Korea. Long-term collaboration with the Royal Netherlands Gymnastics Union for the Miffy exercise certificate

2015 Miffy celebrates her 60th anniversary. *Dick Bruna. Artist*

opens at the Rijksmuseum. Sixty
international artists each decorate
a 1.80-metre-high Miffy statue for
the Miffy Art Parade, all of which
are exhibited and auctioned for
UNICEF. Miffy is the mascot for
Le Grand Depart of the 2015 Tour
de France in Utrecht. *The Studio:
Dick Bruna* is housed within
the Centraal Museum, an exact
replica of Bruna's art studio where
he worked for many decades

2016 Dick Bruna House in Utrecht
reopens as Miffy Museum.

Awarded the Max Velthuijs Prize,
a lifetime achievement award
for children's book illustrators,
presented once every three years

2017 Dies, 16 February

2018 *The Dark Side of Dick Bruna*
opens at the Kunsthal in
Rotterdam, showing more
than 350 original works from
the *Zwarte Beertjes* series

2019 To celebrate the Year of
Rembrandt *Miffy x Rembrandt* is
published in Dutch and English
by Mercis Publishing and the

Rijksmuseum. Exhibition at Albus
Gallery in Seoul, South Korea

2020 Sixty-five years of Miffy celebrated
throughout the world

ACKNOWLEDGMENTS

This is Dick Bruna's book so heartfelt thanks to his family,
Irene, Sierk, Madelon and Marc, and to his second family,
Mercis, especially Karin van Zwieten, Stijn van Grol and Marja
Kerkhof. We are also grateful to the series editors Quentin
Blake and Claudia Zeff, and to the in-house team at Thames &
Hudson of Roger Thorp, Julia MacKenzie and Amber Husain,
for their kindness, patience and attention to detail.

Bruce would like to express his gratitude to Sarah Chalfant
and Luke Ingram at the Wylie Agency for their encouragement
and assistance. Thanks to the Centraal Museum and Miffy
Museum in Utrecht.

Finally, love and thanks to our children, Alvie and Ted.

PICTURE CREDITS

Unless otherwise credited, all artworks are © Dick Bruna and
are reproduced with kind permission of Mercis bv and the
Bruna family.

Photographs on pages 7, 8, 9, 11, 12, 32, 34, 60, 86, 103
Bruna private collection/Mercis bv.

Photographs on pages 24, 81, 82, 83, back cover by Ferry
André de la Porte © Mercis bv.

Photograph on page 99 © Ernst Moritz.

Photograph on page 105 © Martin Godwin.

Every reasonable effort has been made to trace copyright
holders of material reproduced in this book, but if any have
been inadvertently overlooked the publishers would be pleased
to hear from them.

CONTRIBUTORS

Bruce Ingman is an award-winning author and illustrator
and long-time collaborator with Allan Ahlberg on books such
as *The Runaway Dinner*, *The Pencil* and *My Worst Book Ever*.
He is Head of the MA Children's Book Illustration course at
Goldsmiths, University of London and is an ambassador for
the House of Illustration.

Ramona Reihill worked for many years as a children's book
editor, looking after a list that included Miffy. More recently she
has been involved with the creative writing charity *Fighting
Words* as a facilitator and writing mentor.

Quentin Blake is one of Britain's most distinguished
illustrators. For twenty years he taught at the Royal College
of Art where he was head of the illustration department from
1978 to 1986. Blake received a knighthood in 2013 for his
services to illustration and in 2014 was admitted to the Légion
d'honneur in France.

Claudia Zeff is an art director who has commissioned
illustration for book jackets, magazines and children's books
over a number of years. She helped set up the House of
Illustration with Quentin Blake where she is now Deputy
Chair. Since 2011 she has worked as Creative Consultant
to Quentin Blake.

Page numbers in *italic* refer to
illustrations

A. W. Bruna & Zoon 7–8
140 years of *59*
Black Bear series 50–60, *50*, 72, 80
children's books 76
crime fiction series 43
Dick Bruna becomes Art Director 88
Dick Bruna becomes co-deputy
director 88
Dick Bruna joins 35, *35*, 38
Dick Bruna leaves 88
Dick Bruna's covers for 15, *15*, 22,
35–50, 88
Rein van Looy 12
science fiction series 88
Witte Beertjes series 49
Advertisers' Association of the
Netherlands 66
Amnesty International 89
Amsterdam Impressionists 22
Anne-Marie 15, *15*
The Apple 6, 68–69, *68*, 79, *79*, 80

Baldwin, James, *Giovanni's kamer* 48
Bemelmans, Ludwig 101
The Bird 79
Black Bear series, *see Zwarte Beertjes*
Blankenberge 70
Bologna Children's Book Fair *67*
Bons, Jan 88
Boris Bear 89
Boris Bear's Boat 90
Boris in the Snow 91
Brattinga, Pieter 78, 88–89
Breitner, George Hendrik 22
Breukelerveen 11–13, *11*, *12*
Broese bookshop 15, 28
Bruce, Jean
O.S.S.117: De spionne neemt de benen
53
O.S.S.117 te wapen *52*
Schoten vallen in Bangkok *53*
Bruna, Albert Willem (Abs, DB's father)
7, 11, *60*
crime fiction series 43
praise for son's designs 57, 60
reading 43, 49
relationship with Dick 12–13, 15, 22,
35, 57, 60
Bruna, Frederik Hendrik (Frits, DB's
brother) 8
Bruna, Hendrik Magdalenus (DB's
grandfather) 7
Bruna, Hendrik Magdalenus (Dick)
Black Bear series 50–60, *50*, 72, 80
childhood 7–14, *86*, *103*
cover designs for A. W. Bruna & Zoon
15, *15*, 22, 35–50, 88
dinner menu *23*

'drawing with scissors' method 80–81,
81–83
drawings *18*, *19*, *33*, 38–41, *38*, *39*,
40, *92*, *93*
early artwork 11–12, *13*, 15, *16–17*,
19–21
education 10, 14–15, 22
fascination with windows 12, 92
honeymoon scrapbook *36–37*
ill health and death 101–2
influences on 15, 18, 24–25, 28–29,
28–29, 40–41, *41*, 68, 69, 78, 105
and Irene 28, 32–35, *33*, *34*, 38
joins A. W. Bruna & Zoon 35, *35*, 38
leaves A. W. Bruna & Zoon 88
in London 15, 18, 22
love of French music 9, 18, 96
Matisse Chapel of the Rosary 28–29,
68, 69, 92
Mercis bv 89
Miffy series 6, 70–77, 80–88, 89, 91
paintings *13*, *20–21*, *28*, *30–31*
in Paris 15, 18, *19*, *21*, 22, *34*, *36–37*
54, 62
photographs of *7*, *8*, *9*, *24*, *34*, *60*, *86*,
103, *105*
picture books 68–91, 102
posters *27*, 61–67, 89
relationship with father 12–13, 15, 22,
35, 57, 60
Rijksakademie 22
Second World War 11–14
self-portrait *frontispiece*
stamps 89, *101*
studio life 92–102, *94–95*, *96*, *98*
Bruna, Irene (née de Jongh, DB's wife)
6, *33*, *34*
as Dick's 'chief critic' 38, 98
Dick's drawings for *92*, 93, *93*
marriage to Dick 35, 89, 93, 96
meets Dick 28, 32–35
Miffy 70
Bruna, Johanna Clara Charlotte (née
Erdbrink, DB's mother) 7, *7*, 13
Bruna, Madelon (DB's daughter) 80, 93
Bruna, Marc (DB's son) 80, 93
Bruna, Sierk (DB's son)
bedroom 93
his father as a storyteller 96, 98
Miffy 6, 70, 72, 80
Bruna alphabet *100*
Bruna Huis, Utrecht 103
Brunhoff, Jean de 10
Bruun 32, *32*
Burningham, John 101

Caribisch complot (Havank) *59*
Cassandre, A. M. 61, 62
Caviaar en cocaïne (Havank) *58*

Centraal Museum, Utrecht 6, 93, 103
Chisel and Palette exhibition
(1957) *27*
Cézanne, Paul 28
Chagall, Marc 28
Chaplin, Charlie 62
Charteris, Leslie
De Saint in het harnas 43
De Saint stichting 47
The Pirate Saint 54
Ridder Templar 42
The Saint 43, 54
Señor Saint 43
Zijne Hoogheid de Saint 46
Chevalier, Maurice 18
Chisel and Palette exhibition, Centraal
Museum, Utrecht (1957) *27*
Christmas 10, 87, *87*
Circus 80
Clerx, Arnold, *Anne-Marie* 15, *15*
Clichéfabriek, Utrecht 66
collages *28*

Dahl, Roald 101
De Engelenzang mural *29*, *41*
De Rovers (Faulkner) 49
De Saint in het harnas (Charteris) 43
De Saint stichting (Charteris) 47
De Stijl (The Style) movement 24,
78–79, 80
De zaak Louis Bert (Simenon) 45
Dibbits, Taco 91
Disney, Walt 22
Dufy, Raoul 28

The Egg 80
Egmond aan Zee 6, 70
Erdbrink, Johanna Clara Charlotte 7,
7, 13

Faulkner, William, *De Rovers* 49
The Fish 80
Frank, Anne 6

Giovanni's kamer (Baldwin) 48
Golden Lapel Pin of the City of Utrecht
89
Great Wall of China *18*

Havank (Hendrikus Frederikus van der
Kallen) 32
Caribisch complot *59*
Caviaar en cocaïne *58*
De Schaduw 43
Het spookslot aan de Loire 57
Spaanse Pepers 42
Hernhutterschool 10
Het Groene Kruis *64–65*

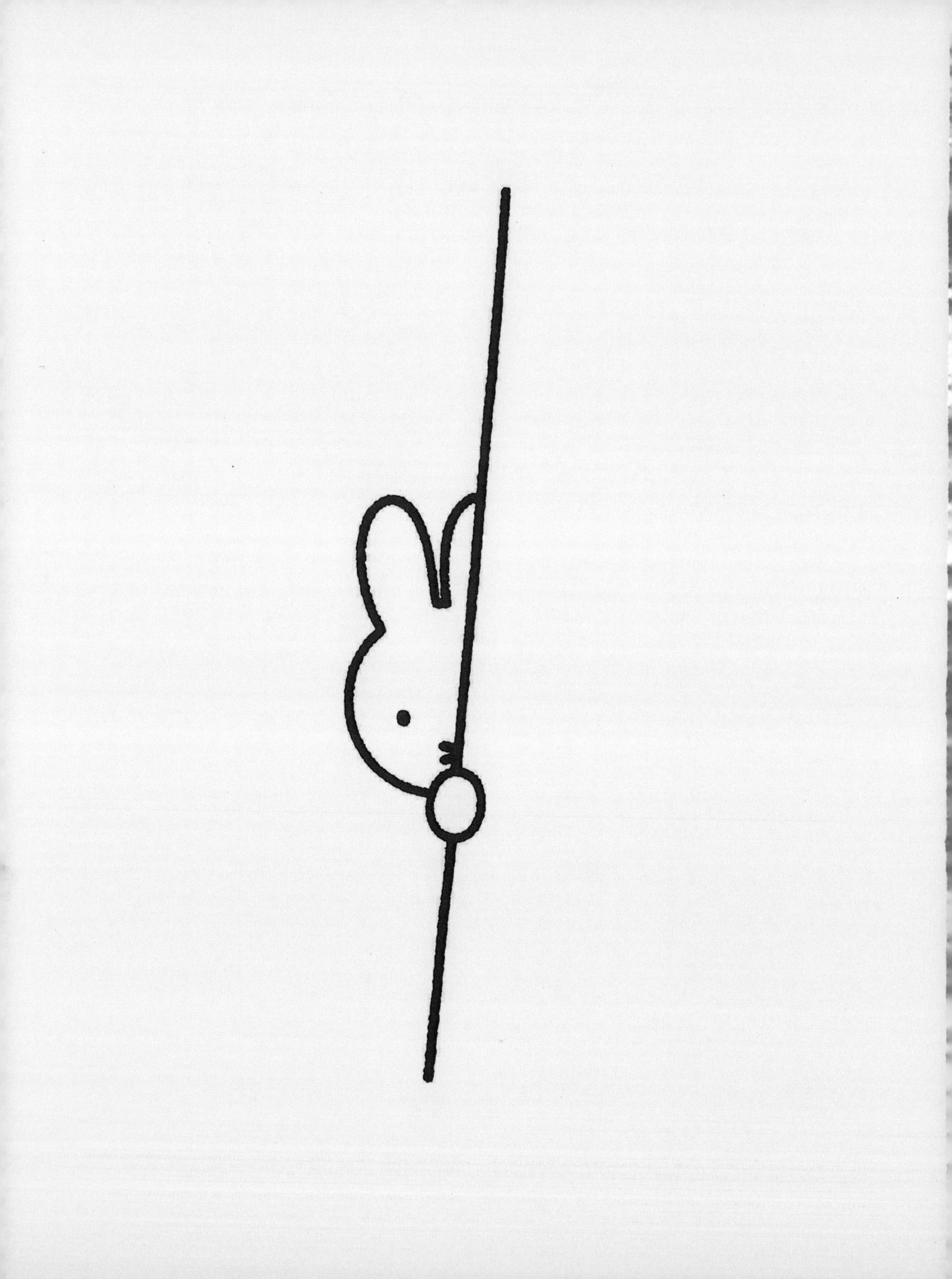